CAMBRIDGE LIBRAF
Books of enduring sch

Literary Stuaies

This series provides a high-quality selection of early printings of literary works, textual editions, anthologies and literary criticism which are of lasting scholarly interest. Ranging from Old English to Shakespeare to early twentieth-century work from around the world, these books offer a valuable resource for scholars in reception history, textual editing, and literary studies.

The Correspondence of Samuel Richardson

Samuel Richardson (1689–1761), the English writer and printer best known for his epistolary novels, including *Pamela* (1740) and *Clarissa* (1748), had preserved copies of his extensive correspondence with a view to its eventual publication, and these volumes, edited by Anna Laetitia Barbauld and first published in 1804, contain her selection from his papers. Richardson became a printer's apprentice in 1706 and for the rest of his life managed a successful printing business in addition to writing his highly popular and influential novels. After the success of *Pamela*, Richardson regularly corresponded with leading contemporary literary figures including Henry Fielding and Samuel Johnson. The letters provide fascinating insights into Richardson's life and literary and social activities, as well as discussions of current affairs. Volume 3 contains correspondence with (among others) Thomas Edwards, the poet and literary editor, and Hester Mulso (Mrs Chapone).

Cambridge University Press has long been a pioneer in the reissuing of out-of-print titles from its own backlist, producing digital reprints of books that are still sought after by scholars and students but could not be reprinted economically using traditional technology. The Cambridge Library Collection extends this activity to a wider range of books which are still of importance to researchers and professionals, either for the source material they contain, or as landmarks in the history of their academic discipline.

Drawing from the world-renowned collections in the Cambridge University Library, and guided by the advice of experts in each subject area, Cambridge University Press is using state-of-the-art scanning machines in its own Printing House to capture the content of each book selected for inclusion. The files are processed to give a consistently clear, crisp image, and the books finished to the high quality standard for which the Press is recognised around the world. The latest print-on-demand technology ensures that the books will remain available indefinitely, and that orders for single or multiple copies can quickly be supplied.

The Cambridge Library Collection will bring back to life books of enduring scholarly value (including out-of-copyright works originally issued by other publishers) across a wide range of disciplines in the humanities and social sciences and in science and technology.

The Correspondence of Samuel Richardson

VOLUME 3

EDITED BY
ANNA LAETITIA BARBAULD

CAMBRIDGE UNIVERSITY PRESS

Cambridge, New York, Melbourne, Madrid, Cape Town,
Singapore, São Paolo, Delhi, Tokyo, Mexico City

Published in the United States of America by Cambridge University Press, New York

www.cambridge.org
Information on this title: www.cambridge.org/9781108034098

© in this compilation Cambridge University Press 2011

This edition first published 1804
This digitally printed version 2011

ISBN 978-1-108-03409-8 Paperback

This book reproduces the text of the original edition. The content and language reflect
the beliefs, practices and terminology of their time, and have not been updated.

Cambridge University Press wishes to make clear that the book, unless originally published
by Cambridge, is not being republished by, in association or collaboration with, or
with the endorsement or approval of, the original publisher or its successors in title.

The original edition of this book contains a number of colour plates,
which have been reproduced in black and white. Colour versions of these
images can be found online at www.cambridge.org/9781108034098

The remarkable characters who were at Tunbridge

1748 Aug:
1 Dr. Johnson
2 Bp. of Salisbury (Dr. Gilbert)
3 Ld. Harcourt
4 Mr. Cibber (Colley)
5 Mr. Garrick
6 Mrs. Frasi (The Singer)
7 Mr. Nash

Wells with Richardson in 1748. from a drawing in his po[ssession]

8 Miss Chudleigh (Duchs of Kingston)
9 Mr Pitt (Earl of Chatham)
10 A. O... Esqr (The Speaker)
11 Ld. Powis
12 Dutch: of Norfolk
13 Miss Banks
14 Lady Lincoln
15 Mr ..... (Afterwards

Wells with Richardson in 1748. from a drawing in his po[ssession]

8 Miss Chudleigh (Duchs. of Kingston) 12 Dutchess of Norfolk
9 Mr Pitt (Earl of Chatham) 13 Miss Banks
10 A. O. Esqr (The Speaker) 14 Lady Lincoln
11 Ld. Powis 15 Mr. ..... Afterwards

...cession with references in his own writing.

16 The Baron (A German Gamester) 19 Miss Onslow
17 Anonym. (Mr Richardson) 20 Mrs Johnson (The Dr's Wife)
18 Mrs Onslow 21 Mr Whiston.

THE
CORRESPONDENCE
OF
SAMUEL RICHARDSON,
AUTHOR OF
PAMELA, CLARISSA, AND SIR CHARLES GRANDISON,

SELECTED FROM THE
ORIGINAL MANUSCRIPTS,
BEQUEATHED BY HIM TO HIS FAMILY.

To which are prefixed
A BIOGRAPHICAL ACCOUNT
OF THAT AUTHOR,
AND
OBSERVATIONS ON HIS WRITINGS,
By ANNA LÆTITIA BARBAULD

IN SIX VOLUMES.

VOL. III.

LONDON: PRINTED FOR RICHARD PHILLIPS, No. 71,
ST. PAUL'S CHURCH-YARD.

1804.

R. TAYLOR, Printer, Black-Horse Court, Fleet Street.

CONTENTS

OF

VOL. III.

	PAGE
Correspondence with Mr. Edwards	1
———————— Mrs. Klopstock	139
———————— Miss Mulso	159
———————— Miss Westcomb	239
———————— Mrs. Scudamore	324

CORRESPONDENCE

BETWEEN

MR. RICHARDSON

AND

MR. EDWARDS.

TO MR. RICHARDSON.

January 26, 1749.

I FIND, dear Sir, that if I put off my acknowledgments to the author of the divine Clarissa till I can meet with words that will fully express what I think and feel on that subject, I must for ever seem either insensible or ungrateful. Accept, therefore, my best thanks both for what you have done, and what you have not done. Whether it be a milkiness of blood in me, as Shakespeare calls it, I know not, but I never felt so much distress in my life as I have done for that dear girl. It is well for us that you are of a humane and gentle disposition; for you are so absolute a master of the heart, that, instead of swelling it with a noble grief, you could in numberless instances have torn it with intolerable anguish.

I am not without hopes that this excellent work has already had some influence on the town; and cannot help thinking that the approbation with which I am told the tender scenes between Romeo and Juliet were received, above the humorous ones between Benedict and Beatrice, might be owing to impressions made by Clarissa, who has tamed and humanized hearts that before were not so very sensible.

But, great as the merit of Clarissa is, I know you are too well acquainted with the town, not to expect that there will be some who cannot relish her beauties; nor would they if she were, what she is near akin to, an angel from heaven. Some such I have met with, though, I thank God, not many: and as I shall think it the reproach of the age if she is not received not only with approbation, but applause; so I shall esteem it my glory, to be enrolled amongst those knights who will defend the honour of Clarissa against miscreant giants and painims.

In short, you have given me a touchstone by which I shall try the hearts of my acquaintance, and judge which of them are true standard.

I heartily wish you, dear Sir, all the profit from this most charming performance which it deserves: honour you can never want, as long as there is any sense of female excellence left in the kingdom.

I beg my humble service to Mrs. Richardson, your family, and all friends; and am, with the greatest gratitude and esteem,

Your most affectionate and

obliged humble servant,

T. EDWARDS.

TO THOMAS EDWARDS, ESQ.

London, January 9, 1750.

DEAR SIR,

I SEND you inclosed copies of your charming sonnet.

Shall we not see you before you go to reside at Turrick?

Don't let me call the last water you shall pass in your way thither Lethe.

Mr. Cibber has sent to tell me, that he is quite well and longs to see me.

Mrs. Donnellan, Miss Sutton, Miss Mulso, and I, have had much talk about you. It would be very needless to say, it was to your advantage. Mr. Duncombe tells me that Mr. Edwards being spoken of at the Archbishop of Canterbury's table—his Grace asked, if it was *good* Mr. Edwards that they meant. The ladies above named wished you had talked more. But Miss S. did me the distinction of saying

ing she feared that my love for Mr. Edwards made me think very unfavourably of another gentleman, whose first patronage was that of her late father. I said, I valued that other gentleman for his good qualities, and was concerned for his bad.

Ever yours,

S. RICHARDSON.

TO MR. RICHARDSON.

Turrick, Jan. 24, 1750.

DEAR SIR,

MANY waters, my dear friend, have I passed since you parted from us at Ember Court: but in none of them have I found any Lethean quality; and I should be ashamed of myself if all the waters in the world could wash your friendship from my remembrance. That worthy heart, which all who have the least worth in themselves must value, has made too deep impressions on me to be effaced by time or place,—impressions which will last as long as my being. But I have besides many personal obligations to you, which perpetually put me in mind of my benefactor, and you have lately reminded me by a civility which I am quite ashamed of. Why did you give yourself the trouble of printing my lines? But since you have, I will not enjoy alone the benefit of your trouble. I have sent a copy to the Speaker, to put under his print of you; and I design one for Mr. Highmore, who I take it for granted has one of those prints.

Here I was interrupted, and before I could proceed was obliged to make a visit which lasted three days. And now I return to my duty and my friend. So far am I from forgetting you, that I am perpetually thinking with gratitude on your favours, particularly that of introducing me both at Mrs. Donnellan's and Miss Mulso's. The small taste I had of the conversation of the ladies you mention made me long for more, and I had new causes

of

of regret for my leaving London, just at the moment I was going out of it; though I know not whether even this loss be not in reality to my advantage. For, I doubt your friendship had drawn such a handsome picture of me as the original would not answer, and those ladies would have soon found me out.

As to my taciturnity, I own I am not naturally loquacious, especially where I am not acquainted: but at Miss Mulso's our stay was so very short, that there was no time for any conversation; and at the other lady's it turned upon a topic on which it certainly was my place to hear their sentiments, and not to interfere with my own.

The mention of that agreeable conversation naturally puts me in mind of Miss Harriet Byron, a lady who has run much in my head lately, and whom I long to be better acquainted with.

May I presume to mention one thing that occurred to me when I heard her letters read? I do it with fear, lest I should be mistaken in the passage, which I speak to from memory, or wrong in my judgment about it, which I shall vehemently suspect if you differ from me*.

I think you design to represent your gentleman (if you ever do represent him) as virtuous with regard to women; a character which, notwithstanding Mr. Cibber's vivacity, it seems strange that any one should think ridiculous in a christian country. Milton, who was as good a poet and as much a gentleman as he, did not think so, when with a noble warmth of indignation he publicly vindicated himself from aspersions which were cast upon him in this respect by Dr. Hall, Bishop of Norwich, in his zele of opposition against some of his works.

---

* The passages objected to were as follow: 'It may not be thought absolutely necessary, perhaps, to make very nice scrutinies into the past life and actions of the man to whom we have no material objection'........ 'Some little, and but little, extenuation lies for the man who is not ungenerous to the partner of his guilt.....
These passages Richardson expunged.

How

How far the licentiousness of the present age will suffer a virtuous young lady to expect a man of this character, I cannot say, but surely I think she should wish it. If I do not mistake (and if I do I beg her pardon and yours), Miss Harriet seems to give up this point in one passage. Is not this something like giving an indirect toleration to vice? And does it not seem a little indelicacy in a lady's character to take up willingly with the reliques of a passion sated by enjoyment? Not to mention the danger of disagreeable comparisons between her and a first-loved object, should not purity desire to unite with purity? And would it be thought extravagant niceness for a virgin to disdain marriage with a widower? I have often admired the delicacy of Milton, who, when he was reproached by the same antagonist with being a widow-hunter, answers, " I care not if I tell him thus much professedly, though it be the losing of my rich hopes, as he calls them, that I think with them, who, both in prudence and elegance of spirit, would choose

a virgin

a virgin of mean fortunes honestly bred, before the wealthiest widow."

Thus I have shot my bolt. If I have mistaken the case, or the sentiment is too nice for the manners of the present age, I depend on your candour to excuse me. But I must have done, or good Mr. Heberden will chide me for teasing you with long letters.

I am exceedingly obliged to his Grace of Canterbury for the kind mention he made of me : it shall be a spur to make me endeavour to deserve his good opinion. I was extremely concerned that I had not an opportunity of waiting on him before I left town.

Your most affectionate
and obliged
THOS. EDWARDS.

I fear I suffer in Miss Sutton's opinion for Mr. Warburton's sake, as much as she thinks he does with you for mine.

TO MR. RICHARDSON.

DEAR SIR,

I SHOULD be insensible of our common calamity, and regardless of the afflicting hand of Providence, if I did not deeply feel the loss we have sustained by the death of the Prince of Wales; and indeed I do feel more than I can easily express on this melancholy occasion. God preserve the King's life, and keep us from the inconveniences which generally attend a minority!

I give you a great many thanks for your last letter, and for your so kindly executing the commission about the plants, which came very safe through your care: but I am afraid I gave you too much trouble in it. Many thanks too for the mezzotintos: they shall go to none but such as deserve them by a true value of the good original.

I have the same sentiments about Dr. N—'s perform-

performance as you have, and think it a shame that he should get so much more for a bad edition of the Paradise Lost than the divine Milton did for the original: but the blame lies on the great people, who encourage such unable undertakers; which if they would not do, the booksellers must break who employ them. I did give the Doctor a little rap on the knuckles in the appendix to the Canons: but as it would not be worth while to kill dead men, such as your namesake and Dr. Bentley, so I do not think his part in it would yield much diversion. It is a heavy, tedious and unedifying performance, which I imagine must sink with its own weight, if we have any taste left amongst us.

However, have not I work enough upon my hands with the professed critic? whose long-threatened vengeance is probably only suspended, to fall with greater weight on my devoted head as soon as his pictures come from Holland; especially as, I hear, matters are compromised between Mallet and him, and I am left the sole butt of his wrath. Would it not be unpar-

unpardonable rashness in me to provoke more enemies, till I see what will befall me from the resentment of those I already have? For not only the Doctor and his patrons, who by his subscriptions must be not a few, but the whole tribe of booksellers, those exact judges and rewarders of merit, would join against me, like the silversmiths at Ephesus, as an enemy to the craft.

As to what you write about my ever-honoured Spenser, it really gives me a very sensible concern ; and, as he says of his Redcross Knight,

———————I do my stout heart eat,
And waste my inward gall with deep despite ;

for I have seen the proposals : and if the work be executed according to the specimen, poor Spenser will be even worse treated than either Milton or Shakespeare; and they were handled badly enough in conscience. But let me ask you, What can be done in this picture-loving age, when, if a bookseller can but get a few

paltry

paltry cuts to raise the price of a book, people will come-in in shoals to subscribe, be the editor's work ever so carelessly or ignorantly executed? If pictures be, as the popish priests say, the books of the unlearned, one may guess whence this encouragement comes: but the discovery will be no great reputation to our age.

For my own part, I never was master of any edition of Spenser but Rowe's, which, upon my first reading it, appeared to be published in a very hasty and careless manner: a very great number of faults I could discover and correct, without comparing with any other edition. Some time since I borrowed the folio of 1609; but it was not till lately that I could get a sight of the first quarto of 1590, which was published in Spenser's lifetime: and I proposed this summer, if I should have life and health, to collate the three together,—as indeed I have begun to do. From hence one may perhaps get a correct text: but to give such an edition of that charming poet as he deserves, and as is
really

really wanted, now when a great deal of his language is become obsolete,—this is a work not to be done with a wet finger, and is, I doubt, beyond my strength; not to mention the collecting parallel places where he has imitated other authors, a work which Lauder has made me sick of. The making a glossary alone is a work of time, and would require several books which I have not,—nor are they to be had in the country : and I will by no means engage myself to publish a work which I cannot perfect; for I should die with shame to be guilty of such crude unlicked performances as I justly blame in others. In short, I doubt nothing can be done to save our classic authors from such scandalous injuries as we both lament, unless they can be rescued out of the hands of the booksellers, who begin quite at the wrong end of the work. Instead of waiting till they can get a good edition of an author, they procure a competency of cuts, publish proposals, levy subscriptions, and then beat about for an undertaker, no matter whom, the cheaper the better,

better, to perform their part of the contract they have made with the public. Can any thing good, any thing reputable either to themselves or their authors, be the result of such preposterous proceedings? Yet what possible method is there of putting a stop to them? This only I can, and this I do promise, that if Spenser be murdered and I live, he shall not die unrevenged, be the assassin who he will.

As to the other affair about our language, the more I consider it, the more difficulties appear in it; and I am convinced that it is not only above my strength, but perhaps that of any one man. I have many doubts myself, and there are many words that I am not clear how they should be spelled: how then shall I set up for a teacher? The most that I could do would be to throw out a specimen by way of spur to others, who, lighting their links at my candle, may make further discoveries. If what you have, with a few additions, would serve this purpose, and it be thought by my friends worth publishing, I should

I should be glad to contribute what I can towards so desirable a thing as settling our orthography: and indeed I think this would be on many accounts the best method; for I apprehend any change must be brought about by degrees, and in the most gentle manner: people would rise up against a dictatorial edict, and would not at once change their mumpsimus for a new sumpsimus, especially as they can plead custom for their mistakes.

But it becomes me, who have a little reputation to lose, to be very cautious of what I publish, as I doubt not there are who would watch for my halting. You must be my Mentor, to check any vanity that you see rising in me; and you ought to do it, since you have been the innocent occasion of my being in danger. You cannot imagine how I am altered since your last letter. I am grown, like your Lovelace, a foot or two taller, and begin to think I may possibly live in this world after I am dead. Your linnet* twitters most enchantingly. I am

* Miss Mulso.

exceedingly obliged to her for her music, and have endeavoured to chirp to her again as well as I can in the inclosed sonnet*, which I beg you to present to her from me, if you think it worth her acceptance. There is, and I doubt not but you have felt it, there is something more deliciously charming in the approbation of the ladies, than in that of a whole university of he-critics; and if I can deserve their applause, let the sour pedants rail as much as they please,

> "For *theirs* the claim to each instructive tongue,
> And *theirs* the great monopoly of song."

Good night, good Mr. Richardson! Remember me to all your good family, to all your pretty disciplesses, and all friends who inquire after

    Your

      Thos. Edwards.

Turrick, March 30, 1751.
Eleven o'clock—a late country hour.

 * Both the sonnets referred to are printed in Mrs. Chapone's Miscellanies.

TO MR. RICHARDSON.

DEAR SIR, *Turrick, May* 8, 1751.

I Did indeed, my dear Mr. Richardson, I own I did think it a long long month: but I grieved only, I did not complain even in thought; for I knew your great occupations, and I feared your indisposition. Sorry am I to find that my apprehensions were too just; but after this long melancholy season we sure may hope for some spring-like weather, and your hurry of business will soon grow less, and then I will hope that a little retirement, and the air of your agreeable suburbane North-End, will restore you.

While you was thus hindered from corresponding with me, very unluckily all my friends were seized with a retention of ink at the same time; so that for a whole month, and that of such weather as confined me very much within, I had not a single line from any creature, except

except a short scrip from Mr. Cambridge to tell me that he had not time to write. But now the charm is broke, and I begin again to hear the post-boy's horn, which when he brought your letter gave me more pleasure than the huntsman's.

All this while I have been hard at work upon Spenser; but to what purpose except my own private satisfaction? There, however, it will repay me: for every time I read I find new beauties in him; such fine moral sentiments, such height of colouring in his descriptions, such a tenderness when he touches any of the humane passions!—Were but his language better understood, he must be admired by every one who has a *heart*.

But Brindley will go on, there is no stopping him: " *Wilfull will do't, that's his crest*," and all I have for it is to write sonnets against these murderers; which they will mind no more than so many old ballads. Indignation has forced two from me in defence of Milton, which I send you inclosed. In the second Dr. N. is

N. is I think very plainly marked; some perhaps will think too plainly: but though I really believe his faults are more of the head than the heart, the example, as you hint, is bad; and it is for the interest of letters in general that such faults, and against such authors, should not pass uncensured, especially when they claim reward instead of being contented with impunity.

A friend of mine tells me that he has collected a great many passages out of the notes of this new Milton, which are just examples to several of my canons: this, if I meet with the book, and have leisure, may deserve consideration: in the mean time it is a noble testimony to my having fairly extracted those canons, if not only the professed critic, but those also *of his school*, work by those very rules there laid down.

Enough of these graceless editors; let me turn to a more agreeable topic. I am exceedingly glad to hear that you have found your Good Man, for I was informed from

Rochester some time ago that Miss Harriet was very much grown; which made me hope that she was almost ready for him. I long to see her. What pleasures do I lose by being banished to such a distance from you! Yet I live in hope; and as she will be every day improving, my pleasure will be so much the greater when it does come. The mentioning of your Good Man puts me in mind of his and our friends the good Bishops his godfathers. Your silence about my Lord of Oxford makes me fear that you are not yet much the better for his neighbourhood. This ought not to be, and therefore I can hardly think it is: and yet, were it otherwise, you would surely have mentioned some of your frequent interviews.

I love you for your epithets. I was going to say you should have been a poet: but that would have been a blunder indeed; for you are a poet, and a noble one; and were not your genius above dancing in shackles, as Dryden calls it, you would put down all us verse-taggers. *These vamping booksellers!* I thank

I thank you for that, Mr. Richardson; and I thank you too, which I should have done before, for your *daughters of the card-table* in a former letter. But these *vamping* booksellers came in the most lucky season that could be imagined. I had been just reading a paper which I met with at Aylesbury: it was a most puffy preface to proposals published by John and Paul,—of what date I know not, for that was torn off. The name of the book was the Universal Dictionary of Commerce: and the preface-monger, after a long, windy, common-place declamation upon trade, navigation, and merchants' accounts, has this proposal, which, as Prior says, " would make even Heraclitus laugh: "—" That our young British nobility and gentry (in general) would condescend for a year or two to be initiated into the business of a merchant in a well regulated and methodical counting-house." A blessed scheme this! To fill our merchants' houses with a parcel of young, lawless, privileged rakes, to debauch their wives and daughters!

I thank

I thank you for sending me Molly Leapor. How does the town receive her? I am sorry to see the number of subscribers fall so vastly short of what appeared to the other volume. What ignorants we are! If we had but thought of *vamping* her with cuts, we had done the business.

Adieu, my dear Mr. Richardson! Take care of your health, and continue to love

Your

T. EDWARDS.

TO MR. RICHARDSON.

Turrick, June 19, 1751.

I THANK you, dear Sir, for your kind letter of May 27. What do I not owe to your goodness in recommending me to the notice of such ladies as Miss Sutton and Miss Mulso? Let the daughters of the card-table bestow their smiles where they please, so I have the favourable

able opinion of such as love and imitate your Clarissa. I beg you, when you have an opportunity, to present my respects to both those young ladies.

I take very kindly your exhortations to me in regard to Spenser: but there are infinite discouragements in my way; others are engaged in the work, and forwarder in it than I can be: then I suppose some persons or other clame a right to the copy; and if so, it cannot be published without the vampers: and my spirit will neither let me go about begging subscriptions, nor hire myself out as a hackney writer to them. Add to this above all, that I think I feel myself unfit for the work; and indeed I cannot help looking on it as a servile Gibeonitish employment: nor, in my opinion, is the judgment of Mr. Addison wrong (however superficial Mr. Warburton esteems him), who, in one of his Tatlers, will not allow the tribe of editors to rank as learned men, but calls them the lacqueys of the learned. However, we will consider the matter further: but in all events I think I should not be willing to advertise before I were ready to publish, lest any dislike to the work, or other accident, should make me worse than my word.

I am obliged to Mr. Upton for his letter to Mr. West, and beg you to return him my thanks for it. By that pamphlet, and from what I hear passed the other day between Mr. Upton and Mr. Brindley's man, I think it is plain he is about an edition; and if Mr. West, who is so good a judge and so fine an imitator of Spenser, will oversee it, I cannot but think it will be a good one.

You do more kind things than you can remember; for my nephew wrote me word that he received my subscription books of Molly Leapor's poems of you, and that you was so good as to take notice of him on his mentioning my name.

T. EDWARDS.

TO MR. EDWARDS.

Dec. 30, 1751.

MY DEAR MR. EDWARDS,

I DID, indeed, think it long before I heard from you; and I was very apprehensive for your health. I rejoice that the occasion of your silence was, your not reaching home sooner than you did.

The account you give of the desolateness of Turrick at this season afflicts me. Dear Sir, what pleasure would you have given me, could you have prevailed upon yourself to make North-End your London house in the winter; and not to have come nearer the town! All your friends would have come to you there. Glad would they have been to do it. I have a stable for your horses. Your servant would have lain with my gardener near his horses, or in the house. Were my family *down*, I should have room for you. But they are in town; and

I have three or four good rooms, any one of which would be at your service, another at your nephew's, another at your brother's, whose acquaintance I should be glad to cultivate. With what pleasure should I have come down to you! Now I see only one poor little girl, and a cat makes a third; and we look upon each other with glazed yet compassionate eyes. You should have pursued your own diversions. I would not have invaded you. I would have done, as to going down, coming up, as business compelled, as if you had not been there. And the first cuckow-note you had heard, or before, you should, without importunity, have gone to your Turrick. Then had you seen it lively and lovely; the green leaf congratulating you; the birds warbling your welcome; and thus all desolateness of the place avoided. You might have visited now-and-then your good Archbishop at Lambeth; Mr. Wray at Richmond. I would have brought you down newspapers, pamphlets, &c. Now your linnet: now other birds

birds of as fine feathers: your linnet itself a nightingale.—You never heard her sing; did you?

Thus receiving pleasure from your visiting friends, giving it to every one in a high degree..... Bless me, my dear friend, cannot this still be thought of for one month or two of the wintry season?—Order your matters; and try. To me it appears very feasible. And what benefit has a man in being a bachelor, if he cannot choose where he will be, and what he will do? and if he is not as much his friends' man as his own?

My dear, very dear friend,

Your most affectionate and faithful

S. Richardson.

TO MR. RICHARDSON.

Turrick, Feb. 19, 1752.

I HAVE been under a great deal of uneasiness, my dear Mr. Richardson, at not hearing from you all this while. In the mean while I make but a simple figure among your disciples in this neighbourhood, who know that I glory in the honour of your correspondence, when to their frequent inquiries, ' How does good Mr. Richardson do? and when did you hear from him?' I am forced to answer, that I hope he is well, but I have not heard from him in a long long month.

I doubt I must beg you not to let Dr. Heberden see this paragraph, for fear he should accuse me of preferring my own satisfaction and reputation before the health of my friend. But indeed I do not. I would consult all three, and the last in the first place;

place; for though I should be very desirous of long letters, if it suited with your health and leisure; though I much envy some certain ladies on that score; yet where my having that pleasure would any ways encroach on either, I should be contented with the smallest scrip from you, till better nerves and a more vacant hour should enable you more fully to satisfy my longing.

Looking the other day over my memorandums about spelling, it put me in mind of your kinsman's remark on the word *style*. It is ingenious, but not true: the Greek and Latin lexicographers have it with *y*, and the word in the original signifies the bole of a tree, and thence *columna* (a pillar), and many other things which answer that shape. The Greeks I say constantly, and the best Roman authors, (for I had it not from Littleton), spell *stylus* with *y*, nor can I find any such Greek word as στιλος. And, indeed, if we examine it, plausible as the conjecture seems which would derive the word from στιζω *pungo*,

pungo, there is no foundation for it; since writing on their waxed tablets was not performed by puncture, but by plowing up the wax, something after the manner of our etching with aqua-fortis; and hence is that expression so frequent in Tully, and the best Latin writers, *exarare* literas. This operation, though, when the art of writing was improved among them, it was performed with brass or iron styles; yet it is probable that at first they only made use of a small sucker or twig of a tree, which is one of the significations which *stylus* bears both in the Greek and Latin authors.

I mention this, to vindicate the decree of Apollo in that instance: but the plausibleness of the objection is a proof of what I apprehended,—I mean the hazard one runs in giving to fallible opinions the sanction of so great a name. Adieu, my dear friend! commend me to your good family, and to all who love

Your

T. EDWARDS.

TO MR. EDWARDS.

London, Feb. 21, 1752.

MY DEAR MR. EDWARDS,

YOU are right in supposing my delinquency owing principally to a great hurry in business. I have, indeed, been greatly hurried by this short and, as it will be, busy session; and you are not wrong in your kind apprehensions as to my want of health.

What of literary news have I to write to my friend? Nothing worthy of his notice, or that he will not hear from better hands.

Mr. Fielding has met with the disapprobation you foresaw he would meet with, of his Amelia. He is, in every paper he publishes under the title of the Common Garden, contributing to his own overthrow. He has been overmatched in his own way by people whom he had despised, and whom he thought he had vogue enough, from the success his spurious brat Tom Jones so unaccountably met with, to write down; but who have turned his own artillery against him, and beat him out of the field, and made him even poorly in his Court of Criticism give up his Amelia, and promise to write no more on the like subjects.

We have a new play in action, translated from the French of a lady at Paris, by the translator of Horace, Mr. Francis, called Eugenia. But it does not greatly please.

Something of Lord Bolingbroke's is in the press, and may be expected in a few weeks.

The Speaker never sees me but he inquires after you. He is, to appearance, cheerful, and the great as well as amiable man. His Lady I have not seen since their great loss. She bears it heavily. The dear child was *her* constant companion and diversion.

My wife and whole family love you. They speak of you always with pleasure. Mr. and Miss Highmore always inquire of you. That careless girl, who has often set the hearts of young fellows on fire, and warmed herself by it, it, the other day set herself in a blaze with her torturing curling-irons. She has scorched her left-hand and arm, and her neck; for her papers first, and her handkerchief, or neck-kerchief, which is it to be called? took fire, and without a Jove she made herself another Semele. She is, however, in a fair way of recovering from the mischief. Chide her, for a warning to her sex, in verse. Has she not been often warned by her mother against playing with fire?

Your affectionate

and obliged

S. RICHARDSON,

TO MR. RICHARDSON.

Turrick, Feb. 28, 1752.

DEAR SIR,

I TAKE the first opportunity of returning you my thanks for your kind remembrance of the 21st. I am very sorry that my fears were so prophetic, and cannot help lamenting in prose what Miss Mulso has so sweetly bewailed in verse, that your health, which is of consequence to so many people, should be precarious : but God knows what is fittest for us; our part is to submit and adore.

I hope the shortness of the present session will make you some amends for the hurry it has given you; and when you have recovered the fatigue of it, I shall long to hear something of Miss Harriet, whom I left in a suspense that gives me no small uneasiness on her account.

The mention of these two ladies may be a not improper introduction to a commission which I beg leave to trouble you with. I often entertain myself with reading over those charming Odes of Miss Mulso's, and admire them more and more every time I read them. I am so proud of the honour she has done me in one of them, that my gratitude has forced from me another sonnet, (you see how bold I grow upon encouragement,) which I desire you

you to give her; and, in hopes of seeing more of her verses, I have presumed to give her a subject. I send you a copy: but as there is a name in it which you have scratched out of better verses, I have taken the precaution to seal up that which is for Miss Mulso; and if you either sink it, or alter the name to Robinson, or any thing else, I will have the sonnet printed, and hawked about under your window *in terrorem.*

I desire my humble service to Mr. Highmore and Miss. I am very sorry for her misfortune, and doubt it is a subject too serious for verse. But a poet would not suppose the conflagration to have proceeded from the heat of the irons, but from the love-verses which she used on that occasion; and which, as Mrs. Mincing says, make the curls *so pure and so crisp,* that they are often put to that use; and the blaze happening on the left side, he would imagine to be extinguished by the prevalent force of the cold about her heart. But if she has spoiled her hair, it is no jesting matter.

I have

I have not heard from the Speaker, but I am very glad to hear that he is well. I doubt he will feel his loss more in his retirement, where the dear girl was more his play thing.

Adieu! I beg my service to Dr. Heberden, and all who remember

Your
T. Edwards.

TO MR. EDWARDS.

London, March 16, 1752.

Is it kind, my dear Mr. Edwards, to make apologies for the honour you do me, as if you supposed it possible that I should not be delighted with your correspondence?

I have executed your commission to Miss Mulso. She thinks herself greatly obliged to you for your favour. I have told her that if she answers it not, I shall be ready to guess that

that it will be owing to her disrelish of the subject, not the performance: so you must thank yourself for that.

I told Miss Sutton how kindly you took her remembrance of you. She desired her compliments to you. She is sure, she says, you are a good man, though she is far from giving up her old friend, as an old friend. She and a lovely cousin of hers will dine with me here on Wednesday. We shall remember you again and again.

What think you of the following criticism of a lady, on these lines of Pope?

> He sees, with equal eye, as God of all,
> A hero perish, or a sparrow fall;
> Atoms or systems into ruin hurl'd;
> And now a bubble burst, and now a world.

" This thought," says the lady, " appears to me far from a just one, and rather a poetical flight than sound reasoning. It is true, that in the sight of the Supreme Being the greatest of his works may be very inconsiderable, as there

there must be an infinite distance between the Creator and the creature: but still, as he has made unalterable differences between his creatures, and we must suppose, from our notions of his attributes, wisdom, justice, &c. that as by one he knows exactly these differences, so he will by the other act according to them. We cannot think an atom and a system, a hero and a sparrow, to be of equal value in his sight. Besides, we are told to the contrary in Scripture, Matt. x. 31. To us finite creatures objects appear greatly lessened, and confounded, by distance; which I take to proceed from some imperfections in our organs. But it cannot be so with God; and we should take care, when we presume to speak of him, and describe his attributes, not to borrow resemblances from our own imperfect nature, and impute to God the defects of man."

Your ever faithful
S. Richardson.

TO MR. RICHARDSON.

DEAR SIR,

You ask me how I spend my time. I answer, Chiefly at home; partly from the badness of the weather to avoid colds, and partly from my not having a servant's horse,—for I have been again disappointed. When the season will permit I busy myself in my garden, where these late winds have made great havock, by tearing up some trees which were of a size not to be replaced in half an age. Among other mischiefs these tempests have done me, I cannot help mentioning one, as it gave me a real concern, which I know you will not laugh at me for. All this season's labours of the poor rooks are in a few hours quite lost, and both nests and eggs torn out of the trees, and scattered all about the ground. You cannot easily imagine the trepidation and terror they were
in

in during the tempest; but though the winds continue high, they are at intervals busy about repairs, and I hope will lay a fresh stock of eggs with better luck.

This impertinent episode of the rookery interrupted the account I was giving of my employment, which I was going to tell you is chiefly reading the choicest authors my little library affords; which, as they are few, I go over and over again; and indeed I almost read my eyes out. What I write is mostly by way of amusement. I send you a sample by obeying in part the commands of your last letter; for I exhort instead of chiding, and address the advice to the sex in general, since a particular application, if the accident has left marks behind it, might make the lady ridiculous, whom I am really concerned for. I commend it to your candour to do with it what you please, with absolute power of life and death.

Wednesday, March 18*th.*

I come

I come now to the paragraph in your letter where you exhort me to vindicate Pope and Milton from their editors; to which I answer, I do not like fighting-work, unless upon a just and reasonable provocation. Now I think I have not this in either of these cases. As to Mr. Pope, though I had some acquaintance with him, and admired him as a poet, yet I must own I never had any great opinion of him in any other light; nor do I see reason to alter my judgment, from what has appeared of his character since his death. With all his affectation of humanity and a general benevolence, he was certainly a very ill-natured man; and can such a one easily be a good man?

But were I ever so disposed, what can I vindicate? Not the morality of his essays, for I think it very faulty. Mr. Warburton has, indeed, tinkered it in some places to make it look orthodox, but yet it will not hold water: what then will become of it, when these patches are taken off? Would it not be ruining the poet to chastise his commentator? And

as

as to any alterations in the text, who can prove against him, who has all Mr. Pope's papers, what is and what is not genuine? Upon the whole, whatever the consequences may be as to Mr. Pope's reputation, I think he deserves them for his ill-judged confidence; and I fear my attacking Mr. Warburton in his defence would look like spleen and resentment for his unworthy treatment of me, rather than an honest justification of a cause perhaps not very defensible. But I really believe he will not suffer much from his commentator; and that he, as well as a much better man, Shakespeare, will soon get rid of the lumber which at present encumbers them, and emerge to posterity clear of their heavy annotator. And this very much cools the expectations you flatter me with, of what may hereafter be thought of the author of the Canons. That pamphlet has already done for me more than I could reasonably expect. I have in some measure vindicated the reputation of the divine Shakespeare; and (but you must not let Miss

Miss S. hear this) in some measure represented the insolence of his over bearing commentator: and though in this engagement I have been a little bitten by the blatant beast of Spenser, yet I have gained so much of the regard and countenance of so many of the most worthy of both sexes, as makes me ample amends for what I have suffered, or can suffer, in this cause. But I think I should be very much mistaken, if I should depend upon being known to posterity by such a work as this, since, if it should escape the fate which most pamphlets of that size are liable to, of falling into the pastry-cook's hands, it must be in a great measure unintelligible, unless by ill luck the bad edition of Shakespeare, which it was written to expose, should go down to posterity with it.

As to the other gentleman you mention, his case I think is very different: his crime seems to be rather chance-medley than wilful murder; and what he has done, if it proceed not from want of genius, is rather an imposition

sition on his subscribers than an injury to the poet; and perhaps the chief blame ought to be laid on his noble patron, who with ill judgment put him upon the work, and probably solicited subscriptions for him. But were I to undertake the correction of all enormities of this sort, I should be reckoned the scourge of authors, and the ruin of the booksellers, whose whole fraternity would look askew upon me, as Paul Knapton has done ever since the Canons.

As for the Trial, if it be not too small (and I think it not easily practicable to make it much larger on that plan), I am very willing it should be made public, as a specimen of some reformation in our spelling, and to stir up others of learning and leisure to attend to it; for, if any thing is done to the purpose in this matter, it must, I think, be by a number of people. At least, for my own part, I acknowledge I am far from being able to produce a complete system on that head. I am perpetually learning something, and meet with frequent difficulties;

nor do I expect to be quite master of our language before I shall have no longer occasion for it. However, as every little helps, I am willing to contribute all I can towards ascertaining it, for the use of those who shall come after me.

But of this I hope to talk with you ere it be long; for I design to surprise you one of these days at North-End, where perhaps I may have the good luck to find some of your Muses or Graces with you. But my prospect of this pleasure is not so near as that I can fix the time, and therefore I beg it may not hinder my hearing from you when your health and leisure will permit.

The lady's remark, in your postscript, on those lines of Pope, is, I think, very just. I own I always looked upon that passage in the same light; and there is in my opinion as great an objection against another line in the Essay, where speaking of the angels, he says they may

—— show a Newton as we show an ape.

For, what pains soever his commentator may
take

take to cover or disguise the real meaning of the words, the thought I think is false; since none, no not the highest order of beings, can look upon a fellow creature, who has improved the faculties of human reason, and exerted them in the most noble manner,—the pursuit and discovery of truth,—otherwise than with honour and approbation, not in a ridiculous and contemptible light; which is the obvious meaning of the image given us above.

Your
T. EDWARDS.

Turrick, March 20, 1752.

TO MR. EDWARDS.

London, Dec. 23, 1752.

DEAR SIR,

I HAVE been, 'tis true, very much disordered with my usual malady; but am sorry you saw any thing of it in my writing.

I had a providential deliverance with regard
to

to the fire. It was occasioned by the carelessness of a boy, whose business was in the warehouse; and who setting some loose papers in a blaze in the warehouse room behind the parlour, it caught the books, that hung upon the poles, as we call them, just under the ceiling; and, had it not been extinguished, would, in a quarter of an hour more, have destroyed the whole house, and, too probably, the neighbouring houses, because of our multitude of papers, &c. It luckily happened about seven o'clock in the evening. I was at home drinking tea, two young ladies with me; and, I bless God, had presence of mind to give the necessary orders: but twice I gave up all for lost. Had any main beam taken fire, the weight of metal on the upper part of the house would have sunk the whole. I bless God for the great deliverance. What the damage is, I know not yet. It is considerable. The room was crowded with books, and the water d d me more damage than the fire, as the latter was so happily extinguished before it reached any other room than that in which it began. It has put me back in all my business; and I shall not retrieve it of some time yet to come. But I am so thankful for the stop of the fire, and for a deliverance from a total destruction, that I make light of what did happen: and still the lighter, as I was insured, and for the saving of my neighbours.

Your ever faithful
and affectionate
S. Richardson.

TO MR. RICHARDSON.

Turrick, January 1, 1753.

DEAR SIR,

AMONG the secondary duties of this day, I know not how to employ part of it better than in writing to my dear Mr. Richardson, and wishing him and his many happy returns of it.

I heartily

I heartily rejoice at your most providential deliverance from the fire; but I still shudder to think what a terror your family must have been in at the time; and I much fear the effects of this calamity upon your too tender nerves.

You are exceedingly obliging in your kind concern about my health. I am recovered from the cold, which I caught in a little journey I made since I came home; and, I thank God, have the use of my eyes very well again. I will make no comparisons, because, as Dogberry, I think, says in Shakespeare, they are *odorous*:—but I must not have the air of Turrick abused, it is a dry wholesome air, and scarce ever subject to fogs: in short, the chief faults of the place are, its being solitary, and its distance from North-End. I would remedy both these evils if I could; but it is impossible. However, as there is, thank God, some good to be extracted from all the evils of this life, perhaps this solitariness may be physically good for the mind:

mind: it obliges a man to converse with, and therefore consequently to be upon good terms with, himself; it forces him to provide some resources from within, when the outward means of entertainment fail. Nor is it fitting for a man to live in a continual state of dissipation and pleasure, though of the most innocent kind, since it relaxes the mind, and makes it unable to bear up against any adverse events, particularly that great one (if, indeed, that ought to be reckoned among such) which all of us, but I especially in my state of health, ought never quite to lose sight of.

To conclude, my dear friend! Homely though it may be, this is my home; here are my books, and here, all, except my friends, that I can call mine: and, therefore, here chiefly lies my duty; nor ought I, though unfortunately a single creature, to be therefore a vagrant without any fixed habitation, or to dragoon my friends throughout the year. You are exceedingly obliging in your very kind offers: when I can with convenience and propriety, I will

I will trouble you with another visit: in the mean time I do assure you that I have no friends, either in Gloucestershire or any where else, who can or would desire to abate the lest jot of that sincere respect and affection which you must always clame from

Your

T. Edwards.

P. S. Pray tell Miss Chapone that *cobweb* comes from the Dutch word *kopwebbe*, and that *kop* in that language signifies a spider.

TO MR. RICHARDSON.

Turrick, March 5, 1753.

DEAR SIR,

IT gives me great pleasure to hear that our friends are well, and remember me: I am very much obliged to you for the sonnet*; it

* Miss Mulso's.

is very pretty, and would make one wish one's self a Robin for such entertainment. I am glad to be so well countenanced in one of my favourite amusements, for I have been bribing all this winter, in order to get a full concert about me in spring; and have a good number of blackbirds, robins, wrens, and other birds of note, who regularly attend my study-window, morning and evening, for a dole. I shall long for an opportunity of seeing the Ode upon Content. The adventures of Fidelio and Honoria shew that lady to be very capable of writing on that subject.

I thank you for what you mention about the Trial; but I have nothing now to add, unless I were to subjoin a petition against the multiplication of et-cæteras. I have never much loved them ever since I read of the Etcætera-Oath: but I have observed that they have grown upon us within these few years; and though an hundred of them really signify no more than one, the mode has been to string several of them together; and even you have so far complied

complied with the fashion as to use three. But a complaint of this nature, I think, would not come properly from the alphabet, who are the parties in our Trial. There are two other gentlemen, who, I think, likewise ought to be called in order. I mean *viz.* and *to wit:* the latter of them is a constant attendant on lawyers and justices' clerks, and perpetually thrusting himself into business where there is no occasion for him. These and several other irregularities may be worth considering, if any body will join to put a helping hand to the work, which is much too great for one man's undertaking.

I am not a little concerned at what you write about shaking of heads. I shall be very sorry if I have given offence at that house; but as I had the free consent of those equally concerned, and no opportunity of asking it there, I thought there could be no just ground of exception, notwithstanding their extreme sensibility.

  Your most affectionate
    and obliged
      T. Edwards.

TO MR. RICHARDSON.

Turrick, March 31, 1752.

MY DEAR MR. RICHARDSON,

Do you think me as insensible as Mr. Warburton, that you should imagine that it ever came into my head to compare my concert with yours? I hope you know me better. You have it under my hand, that one *linnet* of yours makes sweeter music than all the woodlarks that ever flew. But must I not endeavour to have good small beer, because I cannot get Champaigne?

I cannot help mentioning to you, because I know it will give you pleasure, the good fortune that has fallen to one of your pretty disciples in my neighbourhood, who is a great admirer of Clarissa, and has the author's portrait in her closet. She is the daughter of a yeoman near me, who lived very creditably, but had a great many children, of whom this was the youngest, and consequently her fortune was but small:
but

but she was a fortune herself; pretty, as I said, virtuous, good-tempered, and genteel; had a good ear, and, without learning, sung very agreeably almost any thing that she had once heard. With all these accomplishments, the smallness of her fortune was a bar to her matching with the young men of her rank: but lately a gentleman in possession of a very handsome estate, and who will have a greater; bred up in, and determined to live in, the country; who, as he did not want a fortune, would not choose a wife with the modish accomplishments which generally attend one; has advanced her to a rank which she is fit to adorn, though she was not born to it. Her neatness, modesty, and sweetness of temper, often put me in mind of your Pamela in her single state: but when I visited them lately on their marriage, the likeness was exceedingly striking; the same easy behaviour to all about her, the same unaffected humility towards those whom she was now raised to a level with, and that sort of awful regard for her benefactor which

which you so finely paint in that amiable character, were truly exemplified here. The gentleman, like Mr. B., has the majority against him on this occasion; but he is contented rather to be happy than fashionable.

As I know this history will gratify the benevolence of your mind, I will make no apology for the length of it.

I ask your pardon for so boldly attacking your &c.a's quarters; I own they are well manned, and are defended by a fierce soldier, Ancient Pistol, who, cocking his hat and *exhaling* his bilboa, says, in a voice like thunder, " *And are et-cæteras nothing?*" So I believe we must compromise the matter, and agree upon articles; as thus, " That it be lawful to put as many ets as we find convenient, with a dash after them, &—&—&—&—&c. so that &c. shall be used but once.

I desire my sincere respects to every bird of your charming concert.

Yours,

T. EDWARDS.

TO THOMAS EDWARDS, ESQ.

Turrick, April 21, 1753.

I AM charmed, my dear Mr. Edwards, with your sweet story of a second Pamela. Had I drawn mine from the very life, I should have made a much more perfect piece of my first favourite—first, I mean, as to time.

I formerly shewed Mr. Johnson, author of the Ramblers, some few passages of your Trial in MS. without saying whose it was. You know he is writing a Dictionary, that will be an attempt to bring the English language to somewhat of a standard. I forgot to send him one as I ought to have done, as from myself: but he, two or three days ago, sent me one he had bought, with a few remarks written in it, which I have caused to be transcribed, and to accompany this. I told him that they would receive your thanks, whatever were your opinion of the justice of them, and not your ill-will; for he, intending not offence, was at first shy of being named to you. I send you a copy of the letter he sent with them, notwithstanding the very high and undeserved compliment he makes me in it.

As to my girl's reception at Widcomb, give yourself no concern about it. Mr. Allen was in town about three weeks ago. Of a Saturday, when I was out of town, he called in Salisbury-court, and left a card—" Mr. Allen at Mr. W—'s." On the Monday or Tuesday following I called at Mr. W—'s. They all dined out. I left my name with a servant. A few days after, in company with Mr. Millar the bookseller, I met Mr. W—n in the Strand. I addressed myself to him, though he turned short from me (as by accident I then supposed, not design) to speak to Mr. Millar. I told him, lest the servant should have neglected it, that I did call to pay my respects to Mr. and Mrs. Allen. He answered, with a face all his own, and a voice and manner equally peculiar to himself,

himself, that they were very often abroad. I left him and Mr. Millar together—but could not forbear to think, that this was a discouragement to my calling again. I was abundantly confirmed in this surmise, when I found that Mr. Millar had taken notice to his wife and sister of Mr. W—'s manner of speech and behaviour; and when I was told that he had designed to shew his displeasure to me—my crime is great—he said that I had, in a new edition of Clarissa, reflected upon his friend Mr. Pope, by some passages not in the first (which, by the way, I know nothing of); and that I had had *the insolence* to present one of them to his wife. I did, indeed, present one in the octavo size to that lady; and intended it as a civility to one whom I knew before she was his. Do you, my dear Mr. Edwards, remember any such reflexion on Mr. W—n's friend?

Were I to hope for favours from Widcomb; or, did I greatly value Mr. W—n, I should perhaps be solicitous to set this matter right. But,

But, as it comes to me from a third hand, (though a sure one,) it must rest here at present. Poor Mr. Allen!

Your faithful and affectionate

humble servant,

S. RICHARDSON.

TO MR. RICHARDSON.

Turrick, May 1, 753.

I FIND I have been like the woodcock, who, they say, hides his head in a bush, and then thinks nobody sees him: for I was known it seems in Gloucestershire to be the author of the Trial, before I knew that it was published. However, it cannot be helped, and I must take the consequence. But had I not reason, my dear Mr. Richardson, to be diffident of my plan,

plan, and afraid of the consequence of giving the opinions of a fallible man as the unerring dictates of Apollo?

I thank you kindly for sending me Mr. Johnson's remarks, and am obliged to him for them. I wish, indeed, I could have had his opinion before they were published, for I confess myself to be only a learner, and therefore not fit for the office of teaching; and these matters should be well discussed and examined into before they are decided peremptorily one way or other.

I am not for borrowing of the French any words which we can fairly derive from the Latin, or form from our own stock; for which reason I write *honor, superior*, &c. without taking any notice of the French termination *eur*, and *governer*, as we form *defender*.

*En*croachment I acknowledge is right: but I think we are not obliged to write *en*title; because, though it be not perhaps Ciceronian, yet we may as well go to the word *intitulo*, from whence the French form their *entitler*.

That

That *y* is often the Saxon character of *i*, is agreeable to the Decree, p. 12, 13.

Mr. Johnson's conjecture about the Saxon ʒ is, I think, certainly right; I have observed a proof of it in the name of a village in your neighbourhood, Ealing, which in old deeds is written sometimes Yealing, and sometimes Zealing, which seems a corruption of that character.

Page 16. I think Mr. J. is mistaken; the French write *defense, offense:* but whether they did or not, the derivation shews that we should.

Page 17. Dr. Wallis makes *lest*, which he spells *least*, a conjunction; when we say *least I should do so or so*, it certainly is one; but is it not like *ne* in the Latin, both adverb and conjunction?

Page 21. The objection against the spelling of *farther* is strong; and if by the same licence as we from the Saxon ᚠᛖᚩᚱ make our *far*, and from ᚠᛖᚩᚱᚦᛁᛝ *farthing*, it be not allowable also to write *farther*, we must get the decree reversed,

versed, and restore *u* to his place: but the change of *u* into *a* seems not harder than that of *o* into *e*, which we make in the latter syllable; for the Saxons wrote ꝼuꞃooꞃ.

I cannot recollect the lest ground for the exception Mr. W. takes: the man seems to be eat up with pride and ill nature, and I am afraid his new *riband* will make him still worse. Insolence, did he say? None but the most impudent man living could have used that word, speaking of Mr. Richardson. What would Miss S. say if she were to hear this story?

It is with great pleasure that I can tell you that I hope to see you in about three weeks time, when I shall come up to town about a little business. My stay, indeed, cannot be long; but I hope to see you and the rest of my friends again before the summer is over.

Dear Sir,

Your most affectionate

and obliged

T. EDWARDS.

TO MR. RICHARDSON.

Turrick, Sept. 14, 1753.

DEAR SIR,

I HAVE no patience with these execrable rapparees*. Why were they not hanged in their own country for a more honorable way of robbery, before they had ever heard the name of Sir Charles Grandison? It is hard, my dear Mr. Richardson, that you should have this additional vexation, accompanied too, I doubt, with a very considerable loss, just at the time when you was trying to take a little breath, and unbend yourself after your long fatigues.

And I—what a disappointment have I suffered by their villainy! From what agreeable prospects am I fallen! How near did I think myself to a happiness, which I can never again hope for! since, if by any lucky chance I should ever see you here, which I now can

* The Irish piracy of Sir Charles Grandison.

hardly

hardly flatter myself with, yet I can never again expect to see Mrs. Richardson and Miss, who I doubt were once so near me, that Turrick was scarcely out of your way home, and was the nearest house without a sign that you could bait at; for a neighbour of mine told me last week that he dined at Mr. Aubrey's on Wednesday, and that they expected one Mr. Richardson, with his wife and daughter from Oxford, in the evening. This you may be sure was a great mortification to me, who thought I had taken sufficient precautions to way-lay you before you reached that place, especially as you must have already passed me before I heard the news: otherwise, had I met my friend coming back from Dorton, you would certainly have had me at breakfast with you next morning. On Sunday the dead-warrant from Oxford confirmed the truth of my misfortune.

However, what is past cannot be recalled; and therefore, as Priuli says in Otway,

> Of this, as of a jewel long since lost,
> Beyond redemption gone, think we no more.

Only

Only I cannot help envying Mr. Kennicott the hours he spent with you at Oxford.

I must now, as they say at tables, endeavour to play a good back-game, and make myself amends on you at North-End for what I want of you here; and this I will do as soon as I can.

Yours,

T. EDWARDS.

TO MR. EDWARDS.

London, Sept. 19, 1753.

WHAT! says my dear Mr. Edwards, did we in going to Dorton pass by—were we near Turrick? I inquired at Oxford of the master of the inn (the Angel) to which you directed me, and where we put up; who declared that he knew not either my dear friend or Turrick. Scarce out of our way home! What regret you give me!

me! I was, indeed, in haste to get home : the reason too good. I intended only to dine at Cuddesden, the day after we got to Oxford; then to pursue my way that afternoon to Dorton. But Miss Talbot dining out at the distance of eight or ten miles, I was prevailed upon to stay all night. After breakfast we set out for Dorton; twenty-seven gates to open in our way thither from Cuddesden. Only dined there; set out, and inned at Stoken Church. Set out next morning and dropt my wife at North-End, and hastened to London myself— Seventeen days comprehending my whole excursion.

It is true, my wife and Polly will be difficult to get; but I hope one day to attend myself your commands at your beloved Turrick.

You delight me with the back-game you so kindly intend to play. The winter is not far off. The winter I dread for *you*, if you let it approach too near : for *myself*, on rushing into the public, as I have promised. And these Irishmen! They *do* vex me : for I am informed from

from thence, that they are driving on with five volumes at different presses; and are agreeing with some Scottish booksellers to print them in Scotland, and intend to make the most of their wickedness, by sending copies to France before publication.—What have I done, my dear friend, to be thus treated!

Your

S. RICHARDSON.

TO MR. RICHARDSON.

Turrick, Jan. 28, 1754.

WHAT shall I say to you, my dear Mr. Richardson, for not having written to you in all this time?—My return to Turrick, by the number of visits paid in my way, took up almost as much time as that to London had done, so that I have not been a fort'n-night at home.

The contrast between my late situation, happy in the enjoyment of the company of my friends, and my present solitary circumstances, was too strong for me not to want something to compensate the difference. I therefore called Sir Charles Grandison to my assistance; for the conversation I had had with him at Ember and in town was so broken and interrupted that it had by no means satisfied my longing. And what was the consequence? Why, just the fable of the horse and the man: he whom I called in for an ally became my master, and made me spend with him every leisure hour I could command, till I had again gone through the five books; and had they been fifteen, I must have done so. Charming encroacher! He *shall* be my master—do you only forgive him that he made me seem neglectful of you, when in truth I could not think of any body else. He shall be my master; and it will be my own very great fault, if I am not better for his lessons to the last day of my life. God reward you, my dear Mr. Richardson, both here and hereafter,

hereafter, for those most excellent instructions which you have given the world! You teach us both how to live, and how to die. To live like Sir Charles, and to die like Clarissa, what a full complement of felicity that would be! Accept, my dear friend, my poor but sincerest thanks for the many hours which you have given, and will give me; for I assure you that your works are with me (like the Speaker's roast beef) a standing dish; and though I read them ever so often, I always find something new.

And now will you pardon my vanity if I tell you that I have been suspected by two or three gentlemen (not of Sir Charles's character, you may be assured) of having a hand in this most valuable work? I should have been the meanest of creatures if I had not most explicitly disclaimed the having any share in it, and asserted that you wanted no assistance; but at the same time I own that I could not help being proud of the suspicion.

I have received a very kind letter from the Archbishop,

Archbishop to thank me for my sonnet; and I am more proud of that than our friend Warburton can be of his Doctorship.

Your

Thos. Edwards.

TO THOS. EDWARDS, ESQ.

London, Jan. 31, 1754.

To have been able to obtain the approbation of so good a man, and so good a judge, as Mr. Edwards, of my Sir Charles Grandison, is considered by me as a high felicity. Dear Sir! how much more than the praises of forty others do yours raise me!—So warm! so cordial!—But how much am I obliged to those unknown friends of yours, who have made me so high a compliment as to suppose that you would have written on some of the subjects, as they find them treated in the piece! One cause of mortification only, to me, could have resulted from their surmise. They would have selected the best passages or sentiments, and given them to their valued friend at Turrick, and left to the Printer in Salisbury-court a vast heap of the indifferent, which only could be made tolerable by the selected ones, as I may say, in the lump.

O that you could resolve to publish your pieces in two pretty volumes! Pamphlet-sizes are but the reading of a few months. Perpetuate them as they deserve by making them bound books. Warburton's Shakespeare and Pope's Works would always be accompanied by Mr. Edwards's two volumes; and taste and true criticism would be improved by them.

Dear Sir, resolve upon it, and it will be done. Your Canons, your Sonnets, your Trial of the letter Y, already published, will make one volume, what can be your objection?

Your most affectionate and
obliged humble servant,
S. RICHARDSON.

TO MR. RICHARDSON.

Turrick, Feb. 6, 1754.

LET us hope, my dear friend, but hope with an entire submission to His will who knows what is fittest for us, that the approaching spring will set us both more to rights. You are now got rid of one great concern, by having obliged the world with that excellent work, the burthen of which, added to your other fatiguing employments, I feared would have been too heavy for you. The recess of the Parliament will, I hope, soon come; and then you will be able to enjoy the heart-felt satisfaction of reflecting on the good you have done, and the sincere applauses of all the virtuous of both sexes, the number of which I doubt not but your works will increase. What true, what solid glory is this! how far above the trifling commendations due to any one for correcting mistakes in an old author, which are owing to the carelessness or ignorance of a copyist or a printer; or for tickling the ear with a jingle of rhymes, which perhaps tend rather to corrupt than to mend the heart! O my friend! how little soever the difference is regarded now, it will be found to be very great another day. Happy you, who have *chosen* and so well acquitted yourself of that *good part* which shall not be taken from you! nor shall the merit of it be attributed to the unworthy.

As to what you so warmly recommended to me, I will, my dear friend, consider of it; but there are many difficulties. I did design to leave my verses to be published hereafter, if they should be thought worth it: but I don't think that all of them would make more than a just volume, though added to the Canons,— unless they were to be printed Bolingbroke fashion, which I will never consent to; and to make a medley work of prose and verse by printing them all together will be awkward. Besides, the name of the Canons, which is established,

blished, would be lost in the common one of Miscellanies. But I will at leisure, if my eyes will serve me, transcribe the verses; and we will, as I said, consider of it, and see what can be done.

I send you the Sonnet*, and the Letter which you desired : the last I beg may be seen by few, and copied by none ; lest, if his Grace should hear of it, he should blame my vanity and withdraw his good opinion of me.

I take the liberty to inclose likewise another Sonnet, which, if it should be thought worth publishing, I desire may be inscribed to the author of Grandison ; or, if that may not be, of whatever is the title of the book, and subscribed T. E. You see how ambitious I am. I even wish there were to be a copper-plate made of that other painting of you, that this sonnet might be engraved under it. Adieu! My best respects wait on all friends, wherever they are so good as to remember

Your
THOS. EDWARDS.

* Sonnet to Archbishop Herring.

TO MR. RICHARDSON.

Turrick, March 1, 1754.

YOU have given me, my dear Mr. Richardson, both honour and pleasure, by so kindly indulging my ambitious desire of appearing to the world as an admirer of your excellent work, and the friend of its valuable author. I hope in time your name will be prefixed to these so generally applauded performances; then let mine be subscribed at length to the Sonnets; and so I shall go down to posterity in an advantageous light, and be read by the fair and the good, when pamphlets and pamphlet-like publications are consigned to the grocers and pastry-cooks.

Do not be surprised that I send you a few more of my Sonnets: the truth is, I am sometimes forced to this work for employment. Having nothing else to do all day long, but to read and write, it is often more than my eyes will

will bear. Now and then I am obliged to shut them for relief, and meditate such verses as I can; and my friends will of course be troubled with my reveries: but they should watch me, and not suffer me to out-write myself; a mistake which probably I shall be the last person that will see. The first is to our friend Dr. Heberden: the next is to Mr. Williams the Apothecary of Aylesbury, whom you have often heard me mention; he is a very worthy man, and the oldest acquaintance I have in the world, our friendship beginning when I went to school in this neighbourhood at about seven or eight years old: the last is addressed to an honest man who is my day-labourer, and sexton of the parish:—a very proper gradation, you will say:—the minister indeed is left out:---but he is an absenter, and puts us out to a dry-nurse of a curate,—and so he deserves to lose his turn.

Who is that Miss Nanny Williams* who

---

* Mrs. Anna Williams, a blind lady, whom Dr. Johnson took to live with him.

has published a pretty copy of verses addressed to you in the Gentleman's Magazine of January last? Whoever she be, the girl has a good heart, and writes well. I fancy she comes out of your school. If you know her, I desire my service and thanks to her.

I have lost my good friend Mr. Hampden, whose name you used sometimes to see on my letters. This is the last frank I have of Mr. Browne's. Sir William Stanhope is out of England, and where to go for a new supply I know not: so that I must be for the future less loquacious upon paper; which you will say is hard, since it is the only way a solitary man can talk.—Pray has not the sweet Linnet sung lately? or does she wait till the spring is further advanced?

Be well and happy! My paper is out, and I am

Ever yours,

THOS. EDWARDS.

TO MR. RICHARDSON.

Turrick, May 29, 1754.

HAD I not been a good deal indisposed after my return hither, and obliged ever since to be very chary of my eyes, particularly with regard to writing, I should have much sooner sent my thanks to my dear Mr. Richardson for his favours when I saw him last. I do not love to be complaining; especially of those things which must be expected in the ordinary course of nature: but if I should mention nothing of the cause of my silence, I should seem, what I hope I cannot be, ungrateful to a friend to whom I owe so many obligations. I hurried myself to get down by the day of our election, and, when I came, was not well enough to go in the procession, or to dine with the gentlemen on that occasion. Indeed we had no opposition: but, as I had promised to be there, I thought

I thought myself obliged, if possible, to keep my word. But so much for this chapter.

I very much wonder, how it came to pass that I did not hear a syllable of Mr. Duncombe's performance, till Miss Sally happened to rummage it out among other things for my entertainment that evening which I spent without you at North-End. I have since got it. I hope I am not bribed by the compliment to me, but I think it a very pretty poem. I indeed very much dislike the title, which I could wish he would alter in another edition, and call it the Praise of Women, or by any other name than what it bears; for, not to mention that there can be no such word as Feminiad with an *i* after the *n* formed from *femina*; the Battiad, the Causidicad, and other foolish things which have come out with that termination in imitation of the Dunciad, have given people a surfeit of, and even an aversion to, " omne quod exit in *ad*." But what say the ladies to it ? Will it not produce them ? I wish it might be a mean to persuade them to publish, though without

without names. If they would join to give us a miscellany, it would be a better collection than most we have had, and do honour both to themselves and the sex. In the mean while, could one not possibly get a copy of Miss Farrer's Odes, and Miss Pennington's Farthing? Lady Irwin and Mrs. Wright I had never heard of before; but I live in the country and know nothing. What pity it is that Mr. D. was not acquainted with Miss Talbot! But she must not think to be always unknown. I desire you would give my humble service to her when you see her, and tell her I hope she will give me leave, when I publish my Sonnets again, to inscribe her name to that which I had the honour to address to her. But not a word of what I showed you last, which her declining this proposal, if she does, may give a proper occasion to send her. I am afraid this lady did not canvass zealously for the new interest; for I see by the printed poll, that every creature from Cuddesden voted for Wenman and Dashwood. His Lordship indeed could not interfere;

terfere; but Miss Talbot might without breach of privilege have brought over the squires and their tenants to the true interest of their country. But to be serious: I am sorry to see, as I fear I do, so much hard work cut out for Mr. Onslow against next winter by this scrutiny; for the affair must come before the House, and will probably be heard at the bar; which must necessarily prove a most tedious and tiresome business.

Your ever affectionate
and obliged
Thos. Edwards.

TO MR. EDWARDS.

London, June 12, 1754.

DEAR SIR,

I Hope my dear Mr. Edwards is now perfectly recovered, and rejoicing with his birds in the shades of Turrick.

Your

Your friend Mr. Wray quarrels also with the title of Mr. Duncombe's poem; while his father, a worthy and ingenious man, thus in a letter to me, defends, or rather excuses it. "Perhaps," says he, "your friends would not have quarrelled with the innocent word *Feminiad*, if they had not been disgusted with some particular poems ending with *ad*. The *Iliad* and *Henriade* are of the epic kind. *Feminiad* cannot, indeed, be derived from *femina*; for then it ought to be *Feminade*: which is a disagreeable sound.

"But I think it may be derived from the adjective *femineus*, and should be spelt *Feminead*. The opinion of Mr. Browne being asked before he had seen it, and before it was printed, he said he thought it a very proper title, if there were particular characters in it. The chief objection, in my opinion, is, that it was not clear enough. Perhaps this title would obviate that objection, *The Feminead*, or *Female Genius, a Poem*."

I have told the ladies, that this poem, which

so plainly points them out, ought to produce them—and the rather, as they none of them seem displeased with the author for the honour he has intended them. They know him, and know that he means them honour, and is indeed a very valuable young gentleman. But there is one lady whom you have named, who thinks, as I told her, that she has had an escape. Had she *not* set out for the country the very day I received your favour before me, I would not, for your sake, have told her, that you think it a pity that Mr. D. knew not Miss Talbot. Whether she is blamable or not for wishing to glide on so serenely as she has done for years, I decide not at present; but she sincerely rejoiced that she had not a place in this poem, ingenious as it is.

As it is likely that you will see this admirable lady before I shall, perhaps the leave you bid me ask for your inscribing her name to the sonnet that does her real honour, had better be asked by you in person, than by me formally by letter when I write to her. Yet I think it is only

only asking for a denial, as is often the case between the sexes in still more delicate liberties, which a fine woman had rather forgive when taken, than consent to beforehand.— Innocent ones you may be sure I mean.

The man who depends on contingencies, which the will of women govern, can hardly ever determine, at distance, for himself. Mrs. Delany has run away with Miss Chapone to Ireland, and I am at present uncertain about our journey to fetch Patty home. Let me only know when a visit to you will be most agreeable, and the choice of different times, if possible; and I will, if *possible*, accommodate myself to some one of them.

I am, my dear Mr. Edwards,

    Your most affectionate

        and faithful humble servant,

            S. RICHARDSON.

TO MR. RICHARDSON.

Turrick, July 18, 1754.

I Am quite ashamed, my dear Mr. Richardson, when I reflect how long I have been in debt for your last favour. To confess the truth, after a long confinement at home from indisposition and bad weather, I was glad, upon the change of the season, to take the air as much as I could; and my summer friends being returned with the swallows, I have for some time past lived almost wholly on horseback, or in company, excepting the evenings, which of late I have not found so convenient for writing as I could wish.

I like the title of *Female Genius* for Mr. D.'s poem; and, in my opinion, where there is one good title there is no occasion for an *alias:* but every man has a right to name his own

own child as he pleases: it might, therefore, be impertinent in me to object; though, had I not a regard both for the work and the author, I should not have mentioned any thing of it. To speak frankly, the Dunciad being a mock-heroic poem, Mr. Pope might be justified in giving it a mock-epic name. But I always thought it a piece of affectation in Voltaire to call his the Henriade; a Greek termination does not suit with our modern Gothic names: who could bear a Williamade, Carolade, or Fredericade, at least, in any but a burlesque poem?

I did say, and I do really think, that it is a pity so many fine performances, as you and I have seen written by ladies, should be lost to the world; that the public should be robbed of the pleasure and instruction, and they themselves of the honour of them. Yet, seriously to consider of it, what can one say? Till this world is mended, a lady perhaps may be justified in fearing lest she should be looked upon (as Harriet says) " like an owl among the birds," and should lose more credit among the majority than she can gain with the few.

The

The prejudices against a learned wife (such I mean as are free from pedantry, and neglect not their proper duty to acquire their learning) are absurd, irrational, and often flow from envy; but they are strong, inveterate, and too general. Who then is she who dares step forth to vindicate her sex, and assert their clame to genius, at the hazard of forfeiting all her own hopes of a settlement in the world, and friendship with the rest of her sex? I think the present more liberal education of our girls may probably pave the way for their emancipation hereafter : but in the mean time I acknowledge, I cannot from my heart blame those who are afraid of being made the jest of fools for performances above their comprehension. This I know has been the case of a lady whom we are both acquainted with; which makes me not wonder that she rejoices at being not taken notice of in this poem.

I return you many tkanks for Miss Farrer's Ode on the Spring; it is a charming piece, and must do her honour with all judges. I wish I could see that to Cynthia.

The

The verses from my fair *Pupil**, as she does me the honour to call herself, did indeed a little alarm me. To chide me in a sonnet for writing of sonnets, was doing as a physician did by me the other day,—who at the very time he was taking a pinch out of my box reproved me for taking snuff.

But for my Sonnets,—whether I shall ever transgress in that way again I cannot tell; at present I have no impulse to it, and therefore I must beg leave to vindicate or at least excuse myself in prose. The reading of Spenser's Sonnets was the first occasion of my writing that species of little poems, and my first six were written in the same sort of stanza as all his and Shakespeare's are. But after that Mr. Wray brought me acquainted with the Italian authors, who were the originals of that sort of poetry, and whose measures have more variety and harmony in them,—ever since, I wrote in that stanza; drawing from the same fountains as Milton drew from;—so that I was complimented with having well imitated Milton when

* Sonnet by Miss Highmore.

I was

I was not acquainted with his Sonnets. I hope I shall never be ashamed of imitating such great originals as Shakespeare, Spenser and Milton, whom to imitate with any degree of success is no small praise. But why is my writing of sonnets, imitation any more than theirs? At least, it is not imitating them, but the same authors whom they imitated. I have indeed taken the liberty to revive a good old word from them and other of our classic authors, where I could not think of a modern word equally expressive, or to raise the diction above prose. But this has always been allowed lawful, and I wish it were more practised, so it be done with judgment: it would enrich our language with a better ore than we can have from the French mint, which is so much in fashion. If this will not excuse me, I have only to add that the impulse was that way; and to borrow an expression of Mr. Pope's,

> I wrote in sonnet, *for the numbers came;*

and now I submit myself to correction.

Your
T. EDWARDS.

ODE TO CYNTHIA.

BY MISS FARRER.

SISTER of Phœbus, gentle queen,
Of aspect mild, and brow serene;
Whose friendly beams by night appear
The lonely traveller to cheer;
Attractive power, whose mighty sway
The ocean's swelling waves obey,
And, mounting upward, seem to raise
A liquid altar to thy praise:
Thee, wither'd hags at midnight hour
Invoke to their infernal bow'r.
But I to no such horrid rite,
Sweet queen, implore thy sacred light:
Nor seek while all but lovers sleep
To rob the miser's treasur'd heap.
Thy kindly beams alone impart
To find the youth who stole my heart,
And guide me from thy silver throne
To steal *his* heart, or *find* my own.

TO MR. RICHARDSON.

Turrick, August 1, 1754.

I was willing, my good Mr. Richardson, to have made some excuse for the coyness of the dear creatures in the point of owning themselves to be mistresses of talents which really do them honour; but you have beat me out of my defence by your just reasoning, and I acknowledge the wrongness of my partiality for them against themselves,—or, to speak more plainly, for their foible against their true interest. O that you could (and if not you, I know not who can) persuade them to emerge quite, and vindicate their just clame to genius, against the doubters and maligners!

I give you many thanks for that sweet little Ode of Miss Farrer's. I think myself honoured by the trust, and promise that the conditions shall be religiously observed.

I know

I know not how it is, but autumn seems this year to be creeping apace upon us before we have had any summer. The fellow at Manchester was not much out, who got upon a scaffold in the market-place and proclamed that summer was put off till next year. For my part, I had planned out several schemes of making myself happy in the enjoyment of my friends both here and in other places, which have proved abortive hitherto; and now there will not be time enough this season to put them in execution. Among these was a visit which I had promised myself (and indeed given my friends some reason to expect) into Gloucestershire; but I must now lay aside all thoughts of that.

Another most tempting party I fear I shall not have opportunity of accepting. I have strong invitations from a friend at Lee, near Greenwich, to spend a little time with him, and from thence to pay my duty to the Archbishop, and be introduced to Mr. Gilbert West, a gentleman the honour of whose acquaintance

ance I have long desired, and to whose house the Speaker designed to have carried me with him some time ago, had not a slight indisposition prevented him. It grieves me to lose such opportunities, which God knows whether I may ever live to retrieve; but I must, I ought to be contented to do what I can, where I cannot do what I would.

My respects to Mrs. Richardson, to all your dear girls, natural and adopted; and all else who remember

Your

Thos. Edwards.

TO MR. RICHARDSON.

Turrick, Nov. 20, 1754.

MY DEAR MR. RICHARDSON,

WHEN I was at Wrest, I had no leisure for writing: but now I am returned from the palace
to

to the cottage, and fixed in my proper sphere, I cannot help begging for the renewal of your most agreeable correspondence, which has always been one of the greatest reliefs of my solitude. Let me know how good Mrs. Richardson and all your family do; how they like their new habitation, and when you shall be settled in it.

I must not omit congratulating you on your promotion to the mastership of your company, and to wish you through the fatigues of your office as well as possible. The company cannot have a better master, excepting for one part of the duty, and that is the feasting part: and I cannot but figure to myself the miserable example you will set at the head of their loaded tables, unless you have two stout jaw-workers for your wardens, and a good hungry court of assistants. Yours indeed is an example which were the company to follow, your cook's place would be in effect a sine-cure.

I am a good deal uneasy about the winding up of the affair of the letter y, and cannot be satisfied

satisfied with the footing you have put it on: but we will talk more of it when I see you.

Your

T. EDWARDS.

TO MR. EDWARDS.

London, Nov. 26, 1754.

MOST welcome to me is my dear Mr. Edwards's kind invitation to renew the correspondence with him, that has ever been delightful to me.

I was greatly mortified that I could not attend you and the good family at Ember Court. Indeed, the notice was too short. Friday to be told that the post-chaise would be sent for me. The next day, Saturday, my busy day with my workmen, if not prepared by a longer notice!— I was doubly distressed; for my heart was at Ember.

Ember. And how do I know, thought I, but my dear Mr. Edwards, for the sake of an airing, may be in the post-chaise? I thought I could do no less than hire a man and horse, to prevent a trouble that my wishes, could I have gone, would have made probable.

The Speaker was so good as to call upon me at Parson's Green. He liked the house, and situation. O that it could be made your winter-residence, for one, two, or three months!—From thence might you issue at pleasure to reconnoitre your Middlesex and Surrey friends, and London ones too.

My wife is thankful to you for your kind inquiries after her and family. She and her girls have been settled in the new habitation for near a month past; and like it better and better, as they declare, every day.

Miss Mulso and Miss Highmore have visited us there for two or three days. My good Lord of Oxford, and the ladies, called in upon us on Saturday last. All these worthies are in good health, and very much, declaredly, at your service.

service. They hardly ever see me, but your health is one of their inquiries.

Mrs. Donnellan is in tolerable health, and thanks you for your kind remembrance of her. So, I am sure, will Miss Sutton (whom I have not seen for some time) when I tell her of your good wishes.

Nothing, that I know of, is come out, deserving your notice. Dr. Hill is near coming out with his Thoughts of God and Religion, against St. John *. A new Treatise, against the same, is in the press from Dr. Leland.

The *new* Dr. has *not* presented me with his Letters.

My dear Mr. Edwards to congratulate me on the mastership of my company! Nothing escapes him in which his friends have a concern. But you forget, my dear Sir, that I am wicked enough to eat; and am therefore one of those who contribute to the significance and importance of the cook's place.

* Lord Bolingbroke.

The health and happiness you wish to me and mine, constantly attend my dear Mr. Edwards, and all he loves! prays

His zealous friend, admirer, and

humble servant,

S. RICHARDSON.

TO MR. RICHARDSON.

Turrick, Dec. 19, 1754.

I AM very glad to find I was so good a judge of Mrs. Richardson's taste when I assured her she would like your new house when it was fitted up. There are frequently strong prejudices for a habitation which one has been long used to; but when they are once worn out, there can be no comparison between the two situations. May you long live happy there together! but not with all your agreeable daughters: let them be sent off by degrees to plant new colonies, and be only occasional visitors at your agreeable retreat. I, if I live, will sometimes be your guest: but the dead of the winter is not suitable for the visits of an invalid; home is the fittest place for such persons at that season, when excursions to town and about the country are not to be made. Besides, my friends shall have the best, and not the worst of me; to which I must add, that my indisposition would so much the more trouble me, as it would be troublesome to them. Yet think not that I can be easily satisfied without your company: I have it in those excellent works which do honour to the present age, and are a great alleviation of my solitude. People generally keep their cordials for winter. Winter is come, and I fly to mine. Pamela I have lately read, and begun upon Clarissa; and I must still say, the more I read the more I admire: but as I am writing to you I will say no more. What a poltroon is the new-dubb'd Doctor! who, after having received, I will say undeservedly received,

ceived, presents of books from you, which are worth more than all that he has written, or, I am satisfied, ever will write, does not do himself the honour to desire your acceptance of his trifles! But he is all of a piece. For your comfort, Lord R——n is left out too: but that he may thank me for, and so I doubt may you. I wish it were in my power to make you amends.

Dr. Hill's Thoughts I do not expect much from. I doubt they come from the head, and not from the heart. Leland has done very well before, and I hope will not fail now.

I am, my dear friend,

Ever your

T. EDWARDS.

TO MR. EDWARDS.

London, Dec. 30, 1754.

MY wife, my dear Mr. Edwards, bids me, with the compliments of the season, and hearty wishes for your health, tell you, that she, as you foretold, likes her removal to Parson's Green every day more and more; and that she shall like it still better when the house there has been favoured with your residence for some weeks, as opportunity will allow. Your assurance of this, so kindly given, delights us both, and our girls also.

Send them *out* by degrees to plant new colonies!—They are good girls, that's true; but, I am afraid, are neither rich enough, nor handsome enough, to attract lovers. How should I rejoice to see my eldest happily married!

May not my good Lord R——n suppose that the seeming neglect of the new Doctor is owing

owing to his not putting his name to the new production? As for myself, his greatness might well overlook my littleness. He is soon, I hear, to be a Dean—It is thought he will stop there, at least for one while. But from what corner blows his perferment, that he can neglect Lord R——n, if he is not entitled to the excuse I have made for him? I have not read his pamphlet, having expected in it the malice and exultation of an irritated surviving enemy over the ashes of a man (bad as he was!) of whom he was afraid in his lifetime. Has he taken to himself, in the way I mean, the benefit of survivorship? Perhaps I may look into the four proposed letters, when they are completed. But, my dear Sir, reading and writing are become strangely irksome to me; *strangely*, I say, because my habit of making long days gives me more leisure than I have inducement to employ in any way agreeable to myself; so that I seem to be hastening apace into the dozing life of the dormouse. Yet you for a few moments made

made me lift up my drowsy head, and look about me, when you mentioned, in the letter before me, that the poor Pamela, and the persecuted Pamela, had again obtained the honour of your perusal.

I have not read Dr. Hill. Leland's second volume (a very large octavo volume it will be) will be published early in February. *St. John,* as you most properly call him, has raised against his works many writers. I almost wish that they had been left to the noble Discourses of Sherlock, so seasonably published (though not levelled at their author) and to Leland; for the sale is far from answering the sanguine expectations of their boutefeu editor; and I am afraid that so many Tracts on them will add to his profits, by carrying into notice works that would have probably otherwise sunk under the weight of their dogmatical abuse and virulence. I imagine that these works of the quondam Peer, so far as they favour the cause of infidelity, rather abound with objections against the christian system, that *he thought* new, than were

were really so. He seems to have been willing to frame a religion to his practices. Poor man! he is not a doubter now!

Always yours,

S. Richardson.

TO MR. RICHARDSON.

Turrick, Jan. 15, 1755.

MANY, many new years, my dear Mr. Richardson, to you, to Mrs. Richardson, and to all your family! and many thanks to you for alleviating the solitariness of my winter retirement by your kind correspondence! But what beside my thanks can I return you, from a place where I neither hear nor see any thing new to entertain either myself or others? My friends in town do not enough consider, how hungry a countryman is after what passes in the great metropolis, especially if he has spent a great part of his life there, and still has any connexions in it.

I am extremely concerned to hear you complain of being got into a dozing way. Guard, I beg of you, guard against it as much as possible; get into company abroad, or have some at home every evening. How many circles are there of your acquaintance whom you would thus make happy, whom you would enliven and instruct by your conversation, and who would be glad to wait upon you when you cannot come to them! If nothing else will do, you must abate of your laudable custom of early rising, and get as much sleep as you can abed.

As to Miss Sutton's question, I must own I have written no sonnets since I saw you, nor indeed have I had any impulse that way. Whether the vein is exhausted, or whether it is checked by that frost which you know happened last summer, I cannot tell; but I believe I have done with poetry.

How good is Miss Mulso, too, in remembering

bering me sometimes! I beg you to return the compliment with my best thanks to her, and to all your daughters, natural and adopted, who gave me the honour of their notice: it is to your friendship that I owe the favour of so many deserving ladies.

You have a very just idea of St. John's works, and, I imagine too, of the cause of his writing. As far as I have seen, and I read at Ember the last volume, which contains his essays, there is nothing in his objections but what has been published and answered over and over; and I think in several places he contradicts himself. I know not whether his system may be more properly called deistical, or atheistical; since, though in words he allows a God, he seems to make him such a one as Epicurus did; and to think that we are beneath his notice, and have very little or nothing to do with him. He laughs at all notions of revelation, or a particular providence, and reckons the present life the whole of man's existence.

These essays, by the way, afford us abundant
and

and irrefragable proof, that the plan of the Essay on Man was St. John's, and not Pope's; and that however Mr. W— has tinkered it, and by his forced interpretations tortured it into orthodoxy, it was originally founded on fatalism and deism. You have here the whole scheme, the thoughts and in many places the very words of the poem; and a more consistent scheme it is here, than it appears there, after the poet and the parson had laid their heads together to disguise and make it pass for a christian system.

I wish I had the book by me to compare it at leisure with the poem. I am sure, a better prose scheme of it might be extracted from thence than Pope has prefixed to his work. After all, if this is true, as I doubt not, what a man was Pope, to tell us in his preface that he wrote it in verse because he could express *his* thoughts more clearly that way, and afterwards to tell Warburton that *he* understood *his* (Pope's) scheme better than *he himself* did ! which were impossible, if it were indeed
his

his own. And what a man is the note-writer, to defend, and by alterations of the text and forced explications to put off on the world as an orthodox, I mean a christian, system, a piece that really aims at the vitals of religion, by discountenancing the belief of providence and a future state! And yet this very work is the foundation of all his favour with Pope, which was the occasion of all his greatness. Pardon my warmth,—but I do not like dishonesty. However, I have done, and return to your letter.

" That Pamela and Clarissa have again obtained the *honour* of my perusal," do you say, my dear Mr. Richardson? I assure you I think it an *honour* to be able to say that I have read, and as long as I have eyes will read, all your three most excellent pieces at least once a year; and that I am capable of doing it with increasing pleasure, which is perpetually doubled by the reflexion, that this good man, this charming author, is *my friend!* Your works are an inexhaustible fund of entertainment and instruction.

tion. I have been this day weeping over the seventh volume of Clarissa, as if I had attended her dying bed, and assisted at her funeral procession. O may my latter end be like hers! Adieu, my dear friend!

Your most affectionate and obliged
T. EDWARDS.

TO MR. EDWARDS.

January 27, 1755.

HOW unkindly indolent are Mr. Wray, Mr. Cambridge, and *your own* George Onslow, all of them moving in, and curious to know what passes, in the busy world, to suffer their beloved Mr. Edwards to pine after the news they could so easily send him! The first-named I will reproach for his neglect, next time I see him,—if the eel slips not out of my hands before I can speak to him.

We

We have had rumours here of a French war; they have affected our stocks. What a nation of mischievous monkeys is that of France! How I grudge them their country, their climate!—How often am I ready to execrate our Utrecht negotiators!—O that three distinct kingdoms, at least, were erected out of their one!—The whole seventeen Provinces to be one, under a Prince of the Nassau-house!

This abominable Oxford election! What time does it take up! Have you heard of the applause Mr. Pratt has met with from both sides, for his speech for summing up the particulars of the objections to voters for the new interest as it is called, absurdly enough; since it is surely the interest of the country?

Thank you, dear and good Sir, for your advice as to my health. The circles you mention are not, however, so ready, as you kindly imagine, to attend with their comfortings. I am employing myself at present in looking over and sorting, and classing my correspondences and other papers. This, when done,

done, will amuse me, by reading over again a very ample correspondence, and in comparing the sentiments of my correspondents, at the time, with the present, and improving from both. The many letters and papers I shall destroy will make an executor's work the easier; and if any of my friends desire their letters to be returned, they will be readily come at for that purpose. Otherwise they will amuse and direct my children, and teach them to honour their father's friends in their closets for the favours done him.

I have just received the fourth volume of Grandison (having had the preceding three before) from the German translator of that work. At Göttingen they will have it that the piece is imperfect, or suppose that they have it not all.

Our friends at the Deanery frequently inquire after your welfare: Miss T. particularly desires her compliments to you. That excellent young lady, and others whom you know, want to set me at work again. But do you, my my dear Mr. Edwards, occasionally tell them all, that I have been already too voluminous a scribbler; and that I ought to leave writing, while I am well with my friends and favourers.

I am, my dear Sir,

  Your ever affectionate, faithful,

   and obliged humble servant,

    S. RICHARDSON.

TO MR. RICHARDSON.

Turrick, Feb. 4, 1755.

DEAR SIR;

YOUR zeal for me on the occasion of my not hearing from my friends is very kind; but Mr. Wray is not to blame. A large packet of intelligence, both literary and political, which he had sent me about three weeks ago, unfortunately miscarried, I know not by what means, and I have not been able to recover it.

As to Mr. Cambridge, he writes nothing less than a *World:* and Mr. Onslow is, I suppose, so much taken up with parliament matters, that he has no leisure for a country correspondence.

I pretend not to be a politician: but I should imagine the design of the French is only to alarm us, to put us to expence, and to retard our preparations for the colonies. As to an invasion here, I should think, if they did not attempt it at a time when great part of our forces was abroad, and there was a body of six thousand rebels in the heart of the kingdom, it would be a much more hopeless undertaking now. If they have any encouragement to it, it must proceed from that spirit of jacobitism, which is so industriously nursed up and propagated in that university of which Dr. Huddesford, their vice-chancellor, has the impudence to say, that there is not a body of men in England who are more sincerely attached to King George, than the generality of them are. Hardily asserted! But God forbid that the
possession

possession of the present family should ever depend upon their good liking! I hope, by settling the now contested election, the government of the county will be taken out of such hands; and then, by proper care in the distribution of preferments, the spirit of the university may in time be reformed.

As to Miss Talbot's proposal, I must own, I pay a very great regard to her opinion on all occasions, and would carefully weigh and examine my own, whenever I had the misfortune to differ from her. But in the present case I know not what to say. I believe you must be left to yourself, and you will do what is right. I can by no means allow what you say, that you have been already too voluminous; you have not written a letter too much; nor is there the least flagging in your last work; on the contrary, you conclude even with more spirit than you began with. But I think it hardly possible to go beyond what you have done, and I should be extremely jealous of your publishing any thing which should seem to fall short.

short. Nor can I indeed think of any subject that is worthy of you. Mrs. Beaumont's story would, from what I have seen of it, be both entertaining and instructive; but, after what we have been favoured with, would, I doubt, seem uninteresting. I do not in the least distrust your powers, but I fear it will be hard to meet with a subject deserving of your pen. If Miss Talbot can think of such a one, and your health will permit you, the world will have very great obligations to you both. I find our friends in Germany have fallen into the same mistake about the catastrophe of Grandison which a great many unattentive readers have done here; a sign however that they do not think the work too long, since they are desirous of having more of it.

Have you seen the new edition of the Divine Legation, dedicated to Lord Chancellor? Our good friend Dr. Heberden is attacked in a note there with no small contempt. How much am I obliged to that worthy author! If he goes on thus, I shall have company enough, and that of the most deserving sort. I hope however that his honouring me with his friendship is not the cause of the Dr.'s suffering, as it has unfortunately been with others. Yet I cannot think what else can have provoked this Drawcansir against one of the most amiable and inoffensive of men.

Your present amusement is a very laudable one: it will give great pleasure to yourself, and will be an inexhaustible fund of entertainment and instruction to those who come after you. May I flatter myself that some lines of mine will remain in this collection, as a monument to your family of the true friendship and sincere regard I bore to their worthy parent?

Your most affectionate

and obliged

T. EDWARDS.

TO MR. RICHARDSON.

Turrick, March 19, 1755.

I Most sincerely join with you, my dear Mr. Richardson, in wishing that better encouragement were given to, and more care taken of, that brave and useful body of men the British sailors. Can it be so difficult a thing, as one would be apt to imagine from there having been nothing done in it, though the hardships they suffer have been so long and so frequently complained of? I cannot but think that if Sir J. Barnard had exerted his zele and prudence in this cause, instead of opposing the Jew bill, it would have been more becoming both of the patriot and the merchant.

I do not pretend to be a politician: but I own I am more afraid of the French treaties than of their armaments; they never come to an accommodation, but they design only to lull us into

into security, and take us by surprise when we are off our guard upon the faith of their treaties. It was surely a wrong step ever to suffer them to be so powerful by sea; and unless this power be diminished it must necessarily increase by peace and trade; and for aught I can see they must in time become masters of Europe, if they can divide and cajole their neighbors as they have done these forty years past. Execrable indeed (as you justly called them in a former letter) were those peace-makers at Utrecht, who laid the foundation of this grandeur of theirs! and not much less so, our late mismanaging admirals in the affair of Toulon.

If the Oxfordshire dispute should be determined in favor of what is called the new interest, though the decision were made by equity itself, it will be accused of partiality by the losing side; but the feuds raised on the occasion will not, I believe, either be so violent or last so long, as in the contrary case: they will be the last struggles of a dying faction, which can never more hope for victory: the weight of property is considerably on the other side, and is daily increasing; so that from what I have heard, and in part know to be true, if there had been a fair and equal poll, I am satisfied there had been no need either of a scrutiny or a double return. Courage then, my good friend! If we can suppress jacobitism at home, we may the less fear the enemy abroad.

I am very much obliged to you and my other friends who so kindly inquire after my health. I have not much to brag on upon that score. We have had a very long and a very severe winter, with more snow than I can ever remember: what fell last, which is now lingering on the hills as if it waited for more, was very deep, insomuch that a neighbor of mine coming home on foot from Tring perished in it within half a mile of his house, and was not found till two days after. Whether it procede from this severity of the weather, or, as I rather think, from the natural course of my distemper, my breath is shorter than it used to be, be, and my cough worse. Perhaps spring may something relieve me, but I do not much depend upon it. Whether in sickness or health, I am,   Dear Sir,

Ever your

T. EDWARDS.

TO MR. RICHARDSON.

Turrick, May 28, 1755.

IT gives me no small concern, my dear Mr. Richardson, that two long months and more are past since my last to you. I do not remember such a gap in our correspondence since it first began.

Did my situation here afford me materials for writing, though in expectation of a letter every post, and though I had the last word, I should have long since broken this uncomfortable silence: but, alas, I am ill furnished to find my quota of a correspondence, much less can I be able to entertain you wholly from hence on my own small stock.

The Oxfordshire election had been so long depending, that I suppose you in town have been long weary of talking of it; but the determination of that important affair has raised the spirits of all who are the friends of the government thereabouts. We are here in the neighborhood of that infected county, and much the greatest part of the pulpits about us are supplied from thence. The assurance of victory which the leaders of the party had constantly fed them with had made them very bold, and their humiliation now is proportionable: most hang their heads in sullen silence, as conscious that they have more reason to grieve than to complain. The mob, it must be owned, are in some places riotous, to which indeed they are incited by the impudent advertisement of the routed candidates, an advertisement, for which, if the house were sitting, I suppose they would both be sent to Newgate. But I am satisfied the party would have been vastly more outrageous had they been flushed

flushed with victory; and I am informed that in some towns, the inhabitants who were of the new interest must have been in that case obliged to leave their houses, and seek out some other dwellings. Long be remembered the happy victory of St. George's day! a victory which I hope will have a good influence by degrees on every part of the nation.

I have lately read over with much indignation Fielding's last piece, called his Voyage to Lisbon. That a man, who had led such a life as he had, should trifle in that manner when immediate death was before his eyes, is amazing. From this book I am confirmed in what his other works had fully persuaded me of, that with all his parade of pretences to virtuous and humane affections, the fellow had no heart. And so—his knell is knolled.

Your ever affectionate
and obliged
T. Edwards.

TO MR. RICHARDSON.

Turrick, July 28, 1755.

HARD is it indeed, my dear Mr. Richardson, that at this season of the year, when you ought to enjoy repose at Parson's Green, your time should be murdered, and your spirits fatigued, by that worst sort of employment (especially in London) an attendance upon bricklayers! Such a work would be troublesome enough to a man in the highest health and the best spirits, but in your circumstances it is too too burdensome: it is pity you could not get some skilful and honest surveyor to take it off from you.

You very kindly regret the unfortunate solitude of my situation in winter, and judge rightly that my winters are long. I am very much obliged to you, and with all my philosophy cannot help regretting it too, especially of late. I sit and wish, with honest Miss Danby: but, as she says, what signifies wishing? Here my lot is cast; I have no other home; I cannot live in London; nor can I in winter time reap much benefit from neighborhoods, be my situation where it will: the want of domestic society and conversation is my chief misfortune, which in my circumstances is unavoidable: necessary evils we must bear, and we ought to bear them like men: thanks to good Mr. Richardson, I am not a little assisted herein by the frequent perusal of his most useful works.

But you have found out a remedy. How much am I obliged to you, my dear Mr. Richardson, for your most friendly offer, which yet I cannot in honesty accept! Instead of a visiter, who hopes to add to as well as partake in the chearfulness of a friend's family, I cannot think of introducing an invalid, perhaps with the physical tribe following him, and making an hospital of his house to the disturbance both of the principals and servants. Sir Edward Hulse told me once, in an illness which I had in Lincoln's Inn, that bachelors in chambers should

should never be sick. I am sure it may be justly said so of visiters: a man ought certainly to stay at home, whose company will bring much more trouble than he can give pleasure: besides, in winter your family removes to London, and I could not have much of your company, except with such inconvenience to you as would give me pain. But of this we will talk more when I have the pleasure of seeing you at Parson's Green, as I hope I shall some time this autumn.

On account of my health I am obliged to decline acting in the commission for the peace, which is lately come out in this county, where indeed there is great want of acting justices; for I hold it, as Shakespeare says, " *very stuff of the conscience,*" not to undertake an office which I know my health will not permit me in any tolerable measure to perform. I had formerly some difficulties on this subject on other accounts, which I wanted to talk with Dr. Bartlet about; but Providence has superseded that disquisition by this insuperable bar, since it it is needless to inquire whether in such and such circumstances I ought to do what I cannot do at all.

Do not be grieved, my dear friend, at the hints you mention. I do not look upon the event as immediate, but I doubt my time for active usefulness is over. I knew this time must come, and therefore was willing to retire to make some preparation for it; and I thank God I possess my mind with chearfulness, can enjoy myself, and my friend when I meet with one, though I cannot ride a fox chace, or enter upon a new employment, which would demand both a better head and a better constitution than I have at present to engage in it; and if my time for action is over, yet Milton finely teaches me that there is still another duty required of us:

——————————— God doth not need
Either man's work, or his own gifts: who best
Bear his mild yoak they serve him best: his state
Is kingly. Thousands at his bidding speed,
And post o'er land and ocean without rest:
They also serve who only stand and wait.

Adieu,

Adieu, my dear friend! Believe me

Ever your

T. EDWARDS.

TO MR. RICHARDSON.

Turrick, March 19, 1756,
the hills covered with snow.

MY DEAR FRIEND,

How blind are we to futurity! When I was rejoicing that I had so well escaped from the cold I caught in town, and had, some how or other, increased since, the consequences of it were at work in my blood, and a day or two after broke out with such violence, as, I believe, if I had not then reached Aylesbury, would probably have brought me to my grave; but I was happily in the house of a tender friend, as well as a skilful apothecary.

During this illness I received an account from Gloucestershire, that my dear friend Mr. Cambridge

bridge was dead.—That excellent man, whose amable qualities made him loved and respected by all who knew him, whose friendship, approved by an experience of six- or seven-and-thirty years, was my glory and my delight, that excellent man was carried off in eight or ten days by the same distemper that I was labouring under. But he was ripe for glory, and perhaps was taken away from the evil to come.

This stroke was the more surprising to me, as I had but two or three days before received a letter, (which, indeed, had been above a month at Turrick) acquainting me that both he and his lady had got so far through the winter without colds, which used often to confine him for a great while together at that season of the year. Thus my chief connexions with Gloucestershire are broken off at once, and I shall hardly ever again see that county, where I have spent so many happy months. I must own that at my last parting with him I had a sort of presaging in my mind that I should never see him again. I was, I knew not why,

why, very low-spirited all the morning; and after we parted, for he rode some miles on the way with me, we looked back at one another often as long as we were in sight of each other; and when I had lost him, I thought that probably I had taken the last look at him: but I expected the separation would have been made by my death, not by his, who seemed to have better health than when I saw him two years before.

I am exceedingly obliged to you and your good family for your kind wishes for my health; I return you them many fold, and am

Your ever affectionate
and obliged
T. EDWARDS.

TO MR. RICHARDSON.

Turrick, April 15, 1756.

How obliging, my dear Mr. Richardson, is your kind congratulation on my recovery, and

and your tender sympathy on the loss I have sustained by the death of good Mr. Cambridge! that worthy man, to whom all who knew him used to apply the character which Mr. Pope drew for the Man of Ross! Such was his universal benevolence, and his unwearied labour in doing good! And it is something extraordinary that two neighbouring counties should be blessed with two such men. I know, my dear friend, I frequently reflect on, the necessary alternative you mention; and I do not repine; but I must feel,—and indeed if I did not, I should not have deserved such a friend.

As to our circumstances and stations here, God knows what is best for us; and he has kindly mixed its peculiar troubles and inconveniences with every state of life, in order to lead us to him, to wean us from this world, and to urge us to prepare for a better, where alone true happiness is to be found. In the mean time, every one perhaps is apt to imagine that he might be happier in a different state; and notwithstanding I subscribe to the truth
of

of your observation, about the cares which necessarily attend even a happy wedlock, my lonely condition in this declining state of my health sometimes tempts me to such thoughts. But then, on the other hand, it might prove otherwise : so that the safest way is to think that what Providence has ordered is best, and to submit chearfully to my present circumstances.

I am sorry for your additional trouble of removing; I hope however that it is over by this time, and that the ladies are pretty well reconciled to the exchange, which will at lest make Parson's Green more agreeable to them.

I did apprehend that you meant Mr. Pope in that passage in Clarissa that I referred to, and I think that this passage, or another, where you pass a just censure on the satirical charge on the sex in general, " Every woman is at heart a rake,"—one of these, I say, or perhaps both, were what raised the professed critic's indignation so high as to accuse you of abusing Mr. Pope. But how weak, how foolish ! Yet it must be one of these; for, on a careful re-perusal

rusal of the book, there is nothing else in the whole six volumes that can be thought to hint at him.

Ever yours,

T. EDWARDS.

TO MR. EDWARDS.

London, July 12, 1756.

THANK you, my dear Mr. Edwards, for your reproof of me for want of complaisance to my really worthy wife. I read it to her—O how she chuckled! She ever loved Edwards! —And I love that you should Betsey—But, ah these bachelors! They may *afford* to be complaisant to your sex. But I think I will no more complain to Mr. Edwards, child, whoever I tell my tale to!

I have written to Cuddesden, to know when the *hay-harvest* will be over. I am a very cockney: but I shall, perhaps, understand by the answer, when a visit into Buckinghamshire
may

may most conveniently, to certain respectable persons, be extended into Oxfordshire. I hope I shall be able to make the excursion before the summer is over.

You received the militia bill, I hope, as it passed the house of commons.

Have you seen Warton on the genius and writings of Pope? an amusing piece of chit-chat.

Have you seen Johnson's proposals for a new edition of Shakespeare? I will inclose you one of them.

All my family are at Parson's Green. What a profusion of pinks, honey-suckles, lilies, succeed the gaudy ranunculuses there! If change of air, and the exercise, would do you good, how glad should we be to see you there, were it but for one week! Miss Pennington is again with them. Miss Prescott obliged them with her company for some time, and was rewarded with amended health; having been in a bad way before she tried that air.

Miss Westcomb, Miss R—, Miss J—, are well.

well. They desired, when I saw them last, to be remembered to you in the kindest manner. How do all the people I have named love you! Between you and me, I have reason to believe, that Miss Westcomb stays longer in town than she at first intended, for the conveniency of being courted by a very agreeable young gentleman; of whom she has had a very good account—Scudamore his name, of Herefordshire.

Why, why, will not the prudence of our ministers justify our expectations of better success than we have hitherto met with, from our fleets, were it but to furnish one paragraph that might be thought tolerable by my dear friend, in a letter which contains so many of no importance?

Adieu, my dear Mr. Edwards!—God restore you to perfect health! and make your good Mr. Williams his happy instrument to bring about an end so desirable! prays

Your ever affectionate and faithful

S. RICHARDSON.

CORRESPONDENCE

BETWEEN

Mr. RICHARDSON

AND

Mrs. KLOPSTOCK.

TO MR. RICHARDSON.

Hamburg, Nov. 29, 1757.

HONOUR'D SIR,

WILL you permit me to take this opportunity, in sending a letter to Dr. Young, to address myself to you? It is very long ago, that I wished to do it. Having finished your Clarissa, (oh! the heavenly book!) I would have pray'd you to write the history of a *manly* Clarissa, but I had not courage enough at that time. I should have it no more to-day, as this is only my first English letter—but I have it! It may be, because I am now Klopstock's wife,

(I believe

(I believe you know my husband by Mr. Hohorst?) and then I was only the single young girl. You have since written the manly Clarissa, without my prayer: oh you have done it, to the great joy and thanks of all your happy readers! Now you can write no more, you must write the history of an Angel.

Poor Hohorst! he is gone. Not killed in the battle, (he was present at two,) but by the fever. The Hungarian hussars have taken your works, with our letters, and all what he was worth, a little time before his death. But the King of Prussia recompensed him with a company of cavalry. Poor friend! he did not long enjoy it!

He has made me acquainted with all your lovely daughters. I kiss them all with my best sisterly kiss; but especially Mrs. Martha, of whom he says, that she writes as her father. Tell her in my name, dear Sir, if this be true, that it is an affair of conscience, not to let print her writings. Though I am otherwise of that sentiment, that a woman, who writes not thus,

or

or as Mrs. Rowe, should never let print her works. Will you pardon me this first long letter, Sir? Will you tell me, if I shall write a second? I am,

   Honoured Sir,

  Your most humble servant,

    M. KLOPSTOCK.

TO MRS. KLOPSTOCK.

London, Salisbury-court, Fleet-street,
Dec. 22, 1757.

THANKS to you, my dear Mrs. Klopstock, for your exceeding kind and exceeding pretty letter; the first, you tell me, you have written in English. I felicitate you upon it! and also your dear Mr. Klopstock on so precious an acquisition as he has made in such a wife!

 Good Mr. Hohorst! How much was he respected by all mine, as well as by me! And how

how greatly did the news of his death afflict us! Few such soldiers as Mr. Hohorst, I doubt! Pious as brave, had life and opportunity been lent him, he must have shone out the true hero. He used to speak with reverence of his mother. Poor lady! how, if living, does she support the loss of such a son?

He spoke to me of several of his worthy German friends: but from you, dear Madam, I would hope the brief history of your attachments, your pursuits, your alliances.—Happy may you be in all of them!—I was told by two worthy young gentlemen from Gottenburgh, who favoured me with visits when in England, of a sister one of them had, and prided himself in her, because of her many fine qualities, and improving genius. The kind brother of that young lady once wished to introduce me to her: but I never had that happiness. Were you ever in England? If so, were *you* the *single young girl*, you so prettily describe, who since has made M. Klopstock one of the happiest of men?

Let

Let me know every thing a relation would wish to know of my dear Hamburg kindred.

Good Dr. Young, who, with great concern, first gave me an account of Mr. Hohorst's death, has been indisposed for two or three months past; and has been at Bath for four weeks, for the recovery of his health. God succeed to him the use of the waters there! which we hold to be so lenient and salutary. I have transmitted to him the letter you inclosed in that you favoured me with.

You do me honour, Madam, in your approbation of my Clarissa and Grandison.

My daughters receive in the kindest manner, and return with affectionate respect, the sisterly kiss you are so good as to send them;—my daughter Martha most particularly. " O the good Mr. Hohorst!" (exclaimed she, in reading what you mention of the high favour she stood in with him) " How partial to me was he, in the account he gave of me to this good lady! Thank her, dear Sir, in my name, for her opinion, so kindly given in relation to our sex's being ready to make an appearance in print. I am doubly secured from such presumption, by the consciousness of my own want of talents, and by being entirely in this lady's way of thinking in this particular."

You will favour me, Madam, with your farther notice, as above requested. Make my best respects acceptable to your dear gentleman: and allow me to be

Your affectionate friend

and humble servant,

S. RICHARDSON.

TO MR. RICHARDSON.

Hamburg, March 14, 1758.

YOU are very kind, Sir, to wish to know every thing of your Hamburg kindred. Then I will obey, and speak of nothing but myself in this letter.

I was

I was not the lady who hath been with two gentlemen from Göttenburg in England. If I had, never would I have waited the cold ceremony of introducing you to me. In your house I had been before you knew that I was in England. That I shall, if ever I am so happy as to come there. We had a pretty project to do it in the spring to come, but I fear that we cannot execute it. The great fiend of friendship, War, will also hinder this, I think. I fear your *Antigallicans* exceedingly, more than the Gallicans themselves; they, I must confess it, are at least more civil with neutral ships. I pray to God, to preserve you and Dr. Young till peace comes.

We have a short letter of Dr. Young, in which he complains of his health. How does he yet? And you, who are a youth for him, how do you do yourself?

You will know all what concerns me. Love, dear Sir, is all what me concerns! And love shall be all what I will tell you in this letter.

In one happy night I read my husband's poem

poem, the Messiah. I was extremely touched with it. The next day I asked one of his friends, who was the author of this poem? and this was the first time I heard Klopstock's name. I believe, I fell immediately in love with him. At the least, my thoughts were ever with him filled, especially because his friend told me very much of his character. But I had no hopes ever to see him, when quite unexpectedly I heard that he should pass through Hamburg. I wrote immediately to the same friend, for procuring by his means that I might see the author of the Messiah, when in Hamburg. He told him, that a certain girl at Hamburg wished to see him, and, for all recommendation, showed him some letters, in which I made bold to criticize Klopstock's verses. Klopstock came, and came to me. I must confess, that, though greatly prepossessed of his qualities, I never thought him the amiable youth whom I found him. This made its effect. After having seen him two hours, I was obliged to pass the evening in a company, which never had been

been so wearisome to me. I could not speak, I could not play; I thought I saw nothing but Klopstock. I saw him the next day, and the following, and we were very seriously friends. But the fourth day he departed. It was an strong hour the hour of his departure! He wrote soon after, and from that time our correspondence began to be a very diligent one. I sincerely believed my love to be friendship. I spoke with my friends of nothing but Klopstock, and showed his letters. They raillied at me, and said I was in love. I raillied them again, and said that they must have a very friendshipless heart, if they had no idea of friendship to a man as well as to a woman. Thus it continued eight months, in which time my friends found as much love in Klopstock's letters as in me. I perceived it likewise, but I would not believe it. At the last Klopstock said plainly, that he loved; and I startled as for a wrong thing. I answered, that it was no love, but friendship, as it was what I felt for him; we had not seen one another enough to love

love (as if love must have more time than friendship!). This was sincerely my meaning, and I had this meaning till Klopstock came again to Hamburg. This he did a year after we had seen one another the first time. We saw, we were friends, we loved; and we believed that we loved; and a short time after I could even tell Klopstock that I loved. But we were obliged to part again, and wait two years for our wedding. My mother would not let marry me a stranger. I could marry then without her consentment, as by the death of my father my fortune depended not on her; but this was an horrible idea for me; and thank heaven that I have prevailed by prayers! At this time knowing Klopstock, she loves him as her lifely son, and thanks God that she has not persisted. We married, and I am the happiest wife in the world. In some few months it will be four years that I am so happy, and still I dote upon Klopstock as if he was my bridegroom.

If you knew my husband, you would not wonder.

wonder. If you knew his poem, I could describe him very briefly, in saying he is in all respects what he is as a poet. This I can say with all wifely modesty ...... But I dare not to speak of my husband; I am all raptures when I do it. And as happy as I am in love, so happy am I in friendship, in my mother, two elder sisters, and five other women. How rich I am!

Sir, you have willed that I should speak of myself, but I fear I have done it too much. Yet you see how it interests me.

I have the best compliments for you of my dear husband. My compliments to all yours. Will they increase my treasure of friendship?

I am, Sir,

Your most humble servant,

M. KLOPSTOCK.

TO MR. RICHARDSON.

Hamburg, May 6, 1758

IT is not possible, Sir, to tell you what a joy your letters give me. My heart is very able to esteem the favour that you, my dear Mr. Richardson, in your venerable age, are so condescending good, to answer so soon the letters of an unknown young woman, who has no other merit than a heart full of friendship— and of all those sentiments which a reasonable soul must feel for Richardson, though at so many miles of distance. It is a great joyful thought, that friendship can extend herself so far, and that friendship has no need of *seeing*, though this seeing would be cœlestial joy to hearts like ours, (shall I be so proud to say as *ours ?*) and what will it be, when so many really good souls, knowing or not knowing in this

this world, will see another in the future, and be *then* friends!

It will be a delightful occupation for me, to make you more acquainted with my husband's poem. Nobody can do it better than I, beeing the person who knows the most of that which is not yet published; beeing always present at the birth of the young verses, which begin always by fragments here and there, of a subject of which his soul is just then filled. He has many great fragments of the whole work ready. You may think that persons who love as we do, have no need of two chambers; we are always in the same. I, with my little work, still, still, only regarding sometimes my husband's sweet face, which is so venerable at that time! with tears of devotion and all the sublimity of the subject. My husband reading me his young verses and suffering my criticisms. Ten books are published, which I think probably the middle of the whole. I will, as soon as I can, translate you the arguments of these ten books, and what besides I think of them.

The verses of the poem are without rhymes, and are hexameters, which sort of verses my husband has been the first to introduce in our language; we beeing still closely attached to rhymes and iambics.

I suspect the gentleman who has made you acquainted with the Messiah, is a certain Mr. Kaiser, of Göttingen, who has told me at his return from England what he has done; and he has a sister like her whom you describe in your first letter.

And our dear Dr. Young has been so ill? But he is better, I thank God along with you. Oh that his dear instructive life may be extended!—if it is not against his own wishes. I read lately in the newspapers, that Dr. Young was made Bishop of Bristol; I must think it is another Young. How could the King make him *only* Bishop! and Bishop of *Bristol* while the place of *Canterbury* is vacant! I think the King knows not at all that there is a Young who illustrates his reign.

And you, my dear, dear friend, have not hope

hope of cure of a severe nervous malady? How I trembled as I read it! I pray to God to give you at the least patience and alleviation. I thank you heartily for the cautions you gave me and my dear Klopstock on this occasion. Though I can read very well your handwriting, you shall write no more if it is incommodious to you. Be so good to dictate only to Mrs. Patty; it will be very agreeable to me to have so amiable a correspondent. And then I will, still more than now, preserve the two of your own hand-writing as treasures.

I am very glad, Sir, that you will take my English as it is. I knew very well that it may not always be English, but I thought for *you* it was intelligible: my husband asked, as I was writing my first letter, if I would not write French? No, said I, I will not write in this pretty but *fade* language to Mr. Richardson (though so polite, so cultivated, and no longer *fade* in the mouth of a Bossuet). As far as I know, neither we, nor you, nor the Italians have the word *fade*. How have the French found this characteristic word for their nation? Our German tongue, which only begins to be cultivated, has much more conformity with the English than the French.

I wish, Sir, I could fulfil your request of bringing you acquainted with so many good people as you think of. Though I love my friends dearly, and though they are good, I have however much to pardon, except in the single Klopstock alone. *He* is good, really good, good at the bottom, in all his actions, in all the foldings of his heart. I know him; and sometimes I think if we knew others in the same manner, the better we should find them. For it may be that an action displeases us which would please us, if we knew its true aim and whole extent. No one of my friends is *so* happy as I am; but no one has had courage to marry as I did. They have married,—as people marry; and they are happy,—as people are happy. Only one as I may say, my dearest friend, is unhappy, though she had as good a purpose as I myself. She has married in my absence : but had I been present, I might, it may be, have been mistaken in her husband, as well as she.

How long a letter this is again! But I can write no short ones to you. Compliments of my husband, and compliments to all yours, always, even though I should not say it.

M. Klopstock.

TO MR. RICHARDSON.

Hamburg, Aug. 26, 1758.

WHY think you, Sir, that I answer so late? I will tell you my reasons... But before all, how does Miss Patty and how do yourself? Have not you guessed that I, summing up all my happinesses, and not speaking of children, had none? Yes, Sir, this has been my only wish ungratified for these four years. I have been more than once unhappy with disappointments:

but yet, thanks, thanks to God! I am in full hope to be mother in the month of November. The little preparations for my child and child-bed (and they are so dear to me!) have taken so much time, that I could not answer your letter, nor give you the promised scenes of the Messiah. This is likewise the reason wherefore I am still here, for properly we dwell in Copenhagen. Our staying here is only a visit (but a long one) which we pay my family. I not being able to travel yet, my husband has been obliged to make a little voyage alone to Copenhagen. He is yet absent—a cloud over my happiness! He will soon return. . .But what does that help? he is yet equally absent! We write to each other every post. . . But what are letters to presence?—But I will speak no more of this little cloud; I will only tell my happiness! But I cannot tell how I rejoice! A son of my dear Klopstock! Oh, when shall I have him!- It is long since that I have made the remark, that geniuses do not engender geniuses. No children at all, bad sons, or, at the most, lovely

lovely daughters, like you and Milton. But a daughter or a son, only with a good heart, without genius, I will nevertheless love dearly.

I think that about this time a nephew of mine will wait on you. His name is *von Winlhem*, a young rich merchant, who has no bad qualities, and several good, which he has still to cultivate. His mother was, I think, twenty years older than I, but we other children loved her dearly like a mother. She had an excellent character, but is long dead.

This is no letter, but only a newspaper of your Hamburg daughter. When I have my husband and my child, I will write you more (if God gives me health and life). You will think that I shall be not a mother only, but nurse also; though the latter (thank God! that the former is not so too) is quite against fashion and good-breeding, and though nobody can think it *possible* to be always with the child at home!

M. KLOPSTOCK.

TO MR. RICHARDSON.

Hanover, Dec. 21, 1758.

HONOURED SIR,

As perhaps you do not yet know, that one of your fair correspondents, Mrs. Klopstock, died in a very dreadful manner in child-bed, I think myself obliged to acquaint you with this most melancholy accident.

Mr. Klopstock in the first motion of his affliction composed an ode to God Almighty, which I have not yet seen, but hope to get by-and-by*.

I shall esteem myself highly favoured by a line or two of yours or any of your family, for I presume you sometimes kindly remember

Your most humble servant

and great admirer,

L. L. G. Major.

* A subsequent letter contradicts the circumstance of the ode's being written at this time.

CORRESPONDENCE

BETWEEN

MR. RICHARDSON

AND

MISS MULSO.

TO MISS MULSO.

July 13, 1750.

MR. Duncombe has been so good as to leave me at liberty to address myself to dear Miss Mulso, on the blank page of his letter. His great delight is to oblige: and he had reason, from the esteem and even affectionate value he has heard me express for the worthy sister of two brothers, whom I think exceedingly worthy, and for my admiration of what

has

has been communicated to me from her pen, to believe he could not do me a more acceptable favour.

And yet when the power is so kindly, so unexpectedly put into my hands, what have I to say? Power we all wish for, but few know what to do with it.

By endeavouring to acquaint you with what occurs among those in whom you are so deeply interested here in town, I shall possibly best succeed in my wish to entertain you.

Be pleased to know then, that my wife had the favour of a tea-visit from your two good brothers, and from the ever obliging and beautifully-frank Miss Prescott.

But so warm the weather, and Miss Prescott suffered so much by a head-ach, (fine spirits too often pay dearly for them!) that I greatly pitied her; and the more as I saw she would not have had it seen that she ailed any thing. She knows that she was made to give joy to all her friends, and she seemed loth to appear to fail in that principal part of her designation.

They found with me good Mr. Duncombe, and his worthily esteemed son, whom I also found there: for warm, as the weather was, I walked hither from my house in town.

They also found with me, as parts of my own family, the younger Miss Collier, and a daughter of Doctor Allen's of Sion college, who entertained us very agreeably, as well with voices as fingers. Had we had Mr. Mulso's violin, and the voice of his beloved sister, we should have had still greater reason to rejoice in our concert.

Mr. Duncombe mentions to you the verses written by his son, and says they are too many to be inserted in a letter; and so they are. But think you, Madam, that a scribbler must not be vexed, to find that the events of seven tedious volumes are pathetically comprised in a copy of verses of one hundred lines?

We reluctantly parted with our kind visitor at

at between eight and nine; proposing to assemble again in the social winter.

Allow a place, my good Miss Mulso, however unworthy, in the list of your friends, to

<blockquote>Your most faithful

and most obedient servant,

S. RICHARDSON.</blockquote>

TO MISS MULSO.

July 20, 1750.

I CANNOT, dear and good Madam, sufficiently thank you for the favour of yours.

The good Mr. D., whose communicative disposition must ever charm his friends, as what he communicates continually instructs every one who has the pleasure of his acquaintance, had given me more than once a taste of the

the richness of the repasts you furnish out to all whom you honour with your correspondence. But I asked not, nor dared to ask, to be so distinguished. I shall be ever obliged to him for his kind and preventive consideration for me.

But what shall I say of your humility, in the recommendation of a young gentleman to my acquaintance, and for advice; who, not to mention the advantages he must have from the examples of his brothers, and from the precepts of a good father, has, super-added to his own good inclinations, such a sister!

It is, indeed, " a pleasing discovery to me, to find a set of young gentlemen who have spent their lives in London, yet remain untainted with modish vice, uncorrupted by the mean selfish maxims of the world; and who, at the hazard of being laughed at by *men of spirit and fashion*, dare avow and act up to the principles of religion and virtue!"

Excellent Miss Mulso! Were it not for some passages in your letter, in which, from the goodness and kindness of your own heart, you are pleased to express yourself too highly of me, I should adopt and transcribe for you your whole letter. You don't know, I dare say, how excellent a letter it is. Dearly do I love to make young women, especially where there is no danger of pride or conceit, acquainted with themselves. A young lady, who knows her own value, will never do any thing unworthy of herself. She will be her own example.

Your youngest brother brought me this most acceptable favour from you. He stood particularly well with every body at North-End, from the visit paid me there by him, and your eldest brother, by the Mr. D.s, father and son, and the amiable Miss P.

In the praises of every one of these, which all mine overflowed with after their departure, the agreeableness of manners, the modesty of behaviour, the complacency of temper, of this young gentleman, together with the intelligence apparent in his countenance, were taken
great

great notice of. And for myself, I laid myself out to him: I bespoke his acquaintance, and this (it gratifies my vanity to tell you so) before I had the honour of your kind letter, so much in the favour of us both.

On his bringing your letter to me, I renewed my offered acquaintance. He received it with a very agreeable warmth. I look upon it as a favour, and a high compliment (to our tempers at least), when youth will step forward to meet, and accompany, and converse with persons in advanced life. We are bound in return to let them know all that we know of a world *they* are entering upon, and *we* are quitting. And he has given me this very day a fine instance in writing of his genius, and of his kind acceptance of my offered friendship.

But when shall I be acquainted with the other brother, whom you so affectionately describe; both person and mind? Must I stay till you come to town? And must that be still six weeks or two months?

My wife, to whom and her girls I last night read your letter, is your admirer; and will take very great pleasure in cultivating the friendship you so kindly propose to favour her with. I am, Madam,

With very great and affectionate esteem,

Your faithful and obliged servant,

S. RICHARDSON.

TO MISS MULSO.

Salisbury-court, Fleet-street,
July 11, 1751.

I CANNOT, my dear Miss Mulso, say that I am pretty well; but this I can say, that I love you—" as well as ever"—you bid me say— But that is not enough: and yet I loved you the first time I saw you.

I am with you, my dear; and shall be every day, while I am with myself. I only want a description of the room you all generally sit in;

in; then shall I have in view the benign countenance of my good Lord of Peterborough; the benevolent one of his worthy lady; the cheerful one of their venerable mother; the gentle one of the young lady I had the pleasure to see; and the intelligent sweetness shining out in that of my Miss Mulso. Indeed, I revere, I love you all! happy family of harmony and love! My most respectful thanks to my lord and your aunt, for their good wishes and invitation.

" How does your beloved Harriet?" I can't tell how she does. Alas! I have a head that troubles itself not much about her.— " Does not Sir Charles love teasing a little?" No, he does not. Another person, perhaps, may. But it is a fault too ungenerous for Sir Charles Grandison to be guilty of. But here is the thing: you ladies, some of you, scruple not to deserve blame; and then, truly, it is teasing to tell you of your faults in a pleasant way.

Well,

Well, but, after all, I shall want a few unpremeditated faults, were I to proceed, to sprinkle into this man's character, lest I should draw a *faultless monster.* Oh! you have put me into the way: it is but reversing your kind compliment, and making him "more like myself."

" You want this man to suffer as much as Harriet does in suspense." But why so? Is she not the aggressor? Can't she let the man alone? Disliking this man, refusing that, to the number of half a score, she no sooner sees a man whom every body admires for his goodness, and for his personal graces, but he must be hers the moment she sets her eyes upon him! Yes, I warrant! And he is to be punished because he is not captivated by her pretty face, and prattling vein. Has he not been nine years, from seventeen, abroad? Has there not been, in those nine susceptible years, one Harriet to attract him till he saw this? Why will you, my Miss Mulso, pay so ill
a com-

a compliment to the power of your sex, as is implied by your favour to this same parading girl?

But you really and truly would have him to be in love, would you? A wise man to be in love! Tell it not in Gath: lest the daughters of the Philistines triumph. Love of mind, I grant you. Well; and has not Harriet a mind? She has. But Sir Charles has not seen so much of her mind as you have seen. " Well; but he has seen enough to make him admire her, and love her." And so he has. And he has doubtless seen twenty more fine minds, before he saw hers. And he does, moreover, admire and love her for hers. What would you have more? Why, person, I warrant, must be thrown into the scale. Ah! my Miss Mulso!

Well; but, after all, I would not make him guilty of too great refinements: I would draw him as a mortal. He should have all the human passions to struggle with; and those he cannot conquer he shall endeavour to make

make subservient to the cause of virtue. As man should be a reasonable creature; he shall, I think, be made to love like a reasonable man: and the lady will then have reason to rejoice in his love. Because such a love may increase, with her merits, after matrimony: and that will be a security for the virtue, the mental virtue of both. I am apt to believe that there is many a contaminated soul, that has an uncontaminated body to carry it about.

I write to Miss Mulso: and I could not help writing more than I thought I should have had either spirits or steadiness of fingers to write when I began.

Your paternally affectionate,

S. Richardson.

Pray be so good, when you favour me, to leave a margin at sides, top, and bottom:—I am fond of preserving what you write.

TO MISS MULSO.

London, July 27, 1751.
CROSS THING!

"You cannot, you will not, give me a description of the rooms," in which you and your truly worthy friends mostly sit and converse, which I desired you to do, that I might imagine myself now and then among you!—" Come, and see them." Churl!—Yet, in another letter, tell me, that you are so happy, that you dread the coming in of visitors. Very well, Miss Mulso. But you might have gratified me in the requested description; because you could hardly expect that either my disorders or business would permit me to take such a journey.

Could it be done, however, it would be inexpressibly delightful to me to honour myself with the cognition, shall I call it? of my two new nieces. God bless them all three!

You do Clarissa great honour. But I hope you'll get through the last volumes without hartshorn; yet you'll hardly have been able to find an hour to read them in, in which I have not a bottle of it in my hand.

" How could I be so wicked, as to mean to provoke you, and make you saucy?"— Must one be the consequence of the other? Remember, child, where you are.

" You would not give a fig for a man who at twenty-six is too wise to be in love." How unfair is your inference, that the people who boast of philosophy must be those who are born without hearts!

A fine task have I set myself! to draw a man that is to be above the common foibles of life; and yet to make a lover of him! to write, in short, to the taste of girls from fourteen to twenty-four years of age. Let me ask, Did you ever know a girl who in that ten years was not in love either secretly or avowedly? No, say. Well, then, is it not a common failing? It is. And shall a wise
man

man at twenty-six not be able to get above it? Let me tell you, Madam, as the world goes, I think I do a marvellous thing to make a young woman in love with a man of exalted merit. Think you that I don't? And is she to have him with a wet finger, as the saying is? But will you have the story end with a fiddle and a dance: that is to say with matrimony; or will you not? If you will, Harriet must have her difficulties. If not, the dance may be the sooner over, in order to make the happy pair shine in the matrimonial life. And yet you girls generally care not a farthing for the story of an honest couple after the knot is tied.

But set your charming imagination at work, and give me a few scenes, as you would have them, that I may try to work them into the story. You will be in time: for I am not likely to proceed soon with the girl. Only tell me what you will undertake. I expect that you will.

But difficulties must be thrown in. Give me

me half a score of them, Miss Mulso: look but among your female acquaintance, and you will be able to oblige me. Nay, if yourself are a philosopher, and have always been so, I shall judge that you were born without a heart.

"Your pride feels for Harriet." Prettily said! But your pride, my dear, must feel, I doubt, a little more than it has felt. A serene man has great advantages over a girl who finds herself, after roving about in the field of liberty and defying twenty fowlers, just caught. She must part with a few feathers, I doubt. For she will not perch in quiet in her golden-wired cage. But the man shall be rather unhappy, I think, than in fault. How, Mr. R.? But hush. I don't know how I shall order it as yet. Once more; do you set your charming imagination at work, and do it for me.

And here let me own, that you have a manifest advantage over me, in your inference drawn from what I say of Platonic love, and in relation to person; when I cried out, with an

an unjustifiable archness, Ah, my Miss Mulso!
----This was also said to provoke you. And I
submit to your really deserved censure.

" You believe you have been saucy!" You
have not, you cannot be saucy. We are not
upon the argument of filial duty, are we?----
Though never father could be more affectionate
to daughter than I profess myself to be to
Miss Mulso. Witness her

S. RICHARDSON.

TO MISS MULSO.

Sept. 3, 1751.

YOU tell me, my dear Miss Mulso, " that
I am really such a bamboozler on the subject
of love, that you can't tell what to make of
me." Sometimes, say you, I am persuaded

that " you have a noble and just idea of the noblest kind of love; and sometimes I think that " you and I have different ideas of the passion."

In another place, you are offended with the word gratitude: as if your idea of love excluded gratitude.

And further on, you are offended that I call this same passion, " a little selfish passion."

And you say, " that you have known few girls, and still fewer men, whom you have thought capable of being in love."

" By this," proceed you, " you will see, that my ideas of the word love are different from yours, when you call it a little selfish passion."

Now, Madam, if that passion is not little and selfish that makes two vehement souls prefer the gratification of each other, often to a sense of duty, and always to the whole world without them, be pleased to tell me what is? And pray be so good as to define to me, what the noble passion is, of which so few people of
either

either sex are capable. Give me your ideas of it.

I put not this question as a puzzler, a bamboozler, but purely for information; and that I may make my Sir Charles susceptible of the generous (may I say generous?) flame; and yet know what he is about, yet be a reasonable man.

Harriet's passion is founded in gratitude for relief given her in a great exigence. But the man who rescued her is not, it seems, to have such a word as gratitude in his head, in return for her love.

I repeat, that I will please you if I can; please you, Miss Mulso I here mean, (before, I meant not you particularly, my dear, but your sex) in Sir Charles's character; and I sincerely declare, that I would rather form his character to your liking, than to the liking of three parts out of four of the persons I am acquainted with.

You are one of my best girls, and best judges.

Of whom have I the opinion that I have of Miss Mulso on these nice subjects?—I ask therefore repeatedly for your definition of the passion which you dignify by the word noble; and from which you exclude every thing mean, little, or selfish.

And you really think it marvellous that a young woman should find a man of exalted merit to be in love with?—Why, truly, I am half of your mind; for how should people find what, in general, they do not seek?—Yet what good creatures are many girls!—They will be in love for all that.

Why, yes, to be sure, they would be glad of a Sir Charles Grandison, and prefer him even to a Lovelace, were he capable of being terribly in love. And yet, I know one excellent girl who is afraid, " that ladies in general will think him too wise."—Dear, dear girls, help me to a few monkey-tricks to throw into his character, in order to shield him from contempt for his wisdom.

" It

" It is one of my own maxims, you say, that people even of bad hearts will admire and love people of good ones." Very true!—And yet admiration and love, in the sense before us, do not always shake hands, except at parting, and with an intention never to meet again. I have known women who professed to admire good men; but have chosen to marry men—not so good; when lovers of both sorts have tendered themselves to their acceptance. There is something very pretty in the sound of the word wild, added to the word fellow; and good sense is a very grateful victim to be sacrificed on the altar of love. Fervor and extravagance in expressions will please. How shall a woman, who, moreover, loves to be admired, know a man's heart, but from his lips?—Let him find flattery, and she will find credulity. Sweet souls! can they be always contradicting?

" You believe it is not in human nature, however depraved, to prefer evil to good in another,

another, whatever people may do in themselves." Why, no, one would really think so, did not experience convince us that many, very many young women, in the article of marriage, though not before thought to be very depraved, are taken by this green sickness of the soul, and prefer dirt and rubbish to wholesome diet.

The result of the matter is this, with very many young women · they will admire a good man; but they will marry a bad one.—Are not rakes pretty fellows?

But one thing let me add, to comfort you in relation to Harriet's difficulties: I intend to make her shine by her cordial approbation, as she goes along, of every good action of her beloved. She is humbled by her love (suspense in love is a mortifier) to think herself inferior to his sisters: but I intend to raise her above them, even in her own just opinion; and when she shines out the girl worthy of the man, not exalt, but reward her, and at the same

same time make him think himself highly rewarded by the love of so frank and so right an heart.

There now!—Will that do, my Miss Mulso?

I laid indeed an heavy hand on the good Clarissa. But I had begun with her, with a view to the future saint in her character: and could she, but by sufferings, shine as she does?

Do you, my dear child, look upon me as

Your paternal friend,

S. RICHARDSON.

TO MISS MULSO.

Sept. 30, 1751.

I can't say, my dear Miss Mulso, but you have given a very pretty definition of love. I knew that the love you contended for must be a passion fit to be owned; and I am sorry you think there are very few, either men or women, that are capable of it. By the way, I had the generality of men and women in my eye, and not those few, those very few, that are capable of that true love which you call the highest kind and degree of friendship. But do not all men and women pretend to this sort of love? Do not the many, as well as the few, lay claim to this sort of love, and dignify it by the name of a noble passion? And do not all the boys and girls around them, when the passionates (forgive the word) break fences, leap from windows, climb walls, swim rivers, defy parents, say, Such a *furiosa* is in love; ay, and sit down, and form excuses from that single word for the mad-cap! though neither degree, duty, discretion, nor yet modesty, has been consulted in the rapture. Think you, Madam, that a certain monodist did not imagine himself possessed by this purer flame, who, mourning a dead wife of exalted qualities, could bring her to his reader's imagination, on the bridal eve, the hymeneal torch lighted up,

> Dearer to me, than when thy virgin charms
> Were yielded to my arms?

How many soft souls have been made to sigh over the images here conveyed, and to pity the sensual lover, when they should have lamented with the widower or husband!

But the love you describe " cannot be call'd selfish, because it must desire the happiness of its object preferably to its own." Fine talking! Pretty ideas!—Well; and where this is the case we will not call it selfish, I think. And yet

yet what means the person possessed, but to gratify self,—or self and proposed company? Is a man who enters into a partnership to be regarded, who declares that his ardent thirst after accumulation is not for himself, for his own sake; but for his partner's, whom he loves better than himself? or his partner, on the other hand, when he declares the same thing by his partner? This cannot be selfishness, though they combine to cheat father and mother, renounce brother and sister; and having made themselves the world to each other, seek to draw every public and private duty into their own narrow circle. Dear Madam, is not the object pretended to be preferred to self, a single object? a part of self? And is it not a selfishness to propose to make all the world but two persons, and then these two but one; and, intending to become the same flesh as well as spirit, know no public, no other private?

Consider the matter over again, in this its best light. Supposing an opposition founded on reason, from parents or friends, be the flame ever

ever so pure, as well as ardent—It cannot be called furious. Well then, we will not call it so; and yet constitution is a good deal to be considered in this case; the poet tells us,

> Love various minds does variously inspire,
> He stirs in gentle natures gentle fire,
> Like that of incense on the altar laid;
> But raging fires tempestuous souls invade,
> A fire which ev'ry windy passion blows—

And not only constitution, but the fervor or gentleness of the opposition is to be considered: a furious opposition will make a furious resistance. Let passage be given to the gentle stream, and it will glide gently on, and in soft complainings only murmur. But seek to imbank, to confine it, the waters will rise, and carry away the opposing mound; an inundation follows, and then it will roar, and with difficulty be once more confined to its natural channel, a good deal of fair meadow having been overflowed by the attempt to restrain it. But " True love is all tenderness, gentleness, and kindness—".

kindness—" Yes, to the object.—" Ever fearful of offending."—Yes, the object; but nobody else, if withstood.—" And unbounded in the desire of obliging."—The object.—Yes, so it is, whomever else it happens to disoblige.—And this is not selfish!—I am glad of it, with all my heart. How can it?—My dear papa, my dear mamma, my good uncle, my worthy aunt, my loving cousins, and you my old friends, play-fellows, and intimates, I love not myself, though I can give you up, if you oppose my love; for it is Philander that I love; and nobody else. And he loves me, and only me; I for his sake, he for mine: not either for his or her own sake: and do I not give a convincing proof of my disinterestedness when I can throw off all the regards of duty, of interest, of natural affection, for the sake of a man (not for my own sake) whom perhaps I had never seen or known, had I not been at Ranelagh, at Vauxhall, at the Opera, at a certain critical hour, which is to determine the happiness of my whole life? And, as it may happen, your happiness

happiness my dear friends, if your hearts are bound up in me, your grateful Philo-Philander.

But, " true love, you say, cannot be called a sanctifier of bad actions and a debaser of good; or a Moloch deity, which requires duty, discretion, all that is most valuable, to be sacrificed to it; because (love being the highest kind of friendship) there can be no such thing as true love, any more than true friendship, that has not virtue for its basis."—In virtue, I will presume that you include duty; and not only duty, but prudence; and then I will admit that love, such a love, shall be called noble. But you say, my dear, in your former, that very few are capable of such a sort of love. And I, arguing generally, and not to the few exceptions, am not willing that love, indiscriminately taken, should be called noble; because those persons will then shield a passion under the word, of which they ought to be ashamed, when it becomes the Moloch deity, and requires our children to pass through its fires.

" And now, if friendship, infers my Miss Mulso,

Mulso, may be dignified by the word noble, why may not love be allowed an equal claim to the epithet?" I will not, without discussion, without examination, allow it an equal claim, for this plain reason.—Sense may predominate in the one; it cannot in the other. Those will be found to be the most noble friendships which either flame between persons of the same sex; or where the dross of the passion is thrown out, and the ore purified by the union of minds in matrimony. And I am of opinion that love is but the harbinger to such a friendship; and that friendship therefore is the perfection of love, and superior to love: it is love purified, exalted, proved by experience and a consent of minds. Love, Madam, may, and love does, often stop short of friendship.

Love is a blazing, crackling, green-wood flame, as much smoke as flame: friendship, married friendship particularly, is a steady, intense, comfortable fire. Love, in courtship, is friendship in hope; in matrimony, friendship upon proof.

" Cannot

"Cannot all the natural and right affections of the heart, ask you, subsist together?" They can. "Must one absorb and swallow up the rest?" It often does in the greenwood-love I have been mentioning; and yet very frequently itself evaporates in its own smoke, or dies away in embers, warming only its own sticks, and offending every one's eyes and head that sits near it.

"Cannot the same man be at the same time, an effective husband (that is, a married lover), a good son, father, friend, and neighbour?"—He can. "If he can, ask you, what means your question?" This, my Miss Mulso, means my question; that I had before me, love in hope, and not love in proof; love opposed, with reason opposed; and the lovers determined against reason determined. The married lover is an exalted character: but of him we were not debating. We had before us, " two vehement souls, preferring the gratification of each other, often to a sense of duty, always to the whole world, without them;" and

and was I so very great a bamboozler, when I put the question upon the selfishness of souls so narrow and so vehement?

" You did not, you say, mean to exclude gratitude, &c."—I know you did not; and there I own myself to be designedly a caviller; but in pleasantry too, to make you rise upon me, and say right things in your usual beautiful manner. And my end is answered. I suffer. —You shine.

As to the severe things I say of the conduct of " unhappy silly women who have married unworthy men," and all that depends upon these severe things; were not my indignation founded in love of the sex; and had I not an opinion that the cause of virtue and the sex is one; and that such persons betray that of both, I should not be so severe. And these motives make me write so ludicrously sometimes, so angrily at others, on the subject of love; which is really made too generally, nay almost universally, the sanctifier of bad actions.

As to my health—I write, I do any thing I am

am able to do, on purpose to carry myself out of myself; and am not quite so happy, when, tired with my peregrinations, I am obliged to return home. Put me not therefore in mind of myself. My disorder is a chronical one. I am not so bad as I have been.

Adieu, my dear Miss Mulso, child of my heart!

S. RICHARDSON.

TO MISS MULSO.

June 20, 1752.

MY dear Miss Mulso, " won't I let you know when Harriet is married?" And you really expect no back-stroke of fortune? All to be halcyon to the end of the chapter? Think you not that Harriet can shine by her behaviour in some very deep distress*?—Would

---

* About this time, a report was spread that the history of Sir Charles Grandison was to be concluded unhappily.

you,

you, if the thing be ever published, have people be inquiring which is Sir Charles Grandison's house in St. James's Square? and so forth? Poor Sir Charles Grandison! Would it not be right to remove him?—But shall we first marry him?—Shall we shew Harriet, after a departure glorious to the hero, in her vidual glory?—Mother of a posthumous—son, or daughter?----Which----What scenes might be drawn from both circumstances? The case too, so common? Or shall we remove him by a violent fever----or by the treacherous sword of Greville, pretending friendship and reconciliation; and make the assassin a vagabond, a Cain?----What horrors attending the murderer might be painted!----On the very day of the nuptials?----In the vigils of the day so long wished for? or the day before?----Which?---- What distress might be exhibited! What resignation of the hero! What parting scenes drawn!----Harriet, Mrs. Selby, Mrs. Shirley, Mr. Deane, Mr. Selby. Lucy—if on the day ----surrounding the bed of the late blooming, now departing bridegroom?----Lord L. Lord G. and their ladies, sisters so affectionate, and so deservedly beloved, with your favourite Emily (ah the poor Emily!)----all hurrying down, with physicians, surgeons, apothecaries, in all manner of vehicles, in hopes to save the life so precious, or to receive the blessing of the departing saint?----There, my Miss Mulso!---- And the work to be published piecemeal!---- What a surprise would this great catastrophe occasion!----Ladies would, in general, be pleased with it, perhaps----for they love surprises. But, I charge you, my dear! not to talk of this catastrophe to more than select friends!----It will sit the easier upon the heart of my dear Miss Mulso. "She will not cry, like the dear little Emily; because her grief, as her joy, on the reverse of such a catastrophe, will be moderated by some odd notions that have taken hold of her."

"You will say no more of Clementina!"---- What would be her sufferings from marrying a man indifferent to her, to the loss of such a friend?

friend?----his soul at least endangered, as her piety would teach her to apprehend, departing without the pale.----Jeronymo's wounds breaking out afresh----The count and countess----But there would be no end of the complicated woe!----You think I have a talent at such scenes.----Who would not pursue, who can resist his talents?----How would undertakers clap their dragons' wings in different climates, on such events as these!----Your puling love scenes----And girls made unhappy, because they have not this man, or that man. What would be this distress, to that which might be drawn, and a bold word!----will, if I please!----

" Gone to Peterborough!"----Why, yes, they are: and just come back. And to heighten the distress, in case of the grand catastrophe above hinted at, I am endeavouring to draw the hero making love (" with his divided heart!" Naughty girl! When you get notions into your head, there is no getting them out!) Person but just peeping out, in the almost intellectual passion between them. These scenes the sur
viving

viving Harriet may recollect without a blush, the hero departing before her eyes! And will not that be painting, if properly coloured?

You are kind to me, in loving Mr. Duncombe for giving opening to the correspondence between us. He is, for his communicativeness, and for every other good quality, a great favourite of mine. But he is dear to me as a brother, on his introducing my pen to your eye; which brought me so rich a return; from a store sweeter than that of Hybla.

But pray, my dear, before I go any further, remember, I expect from you a short preface for my piece. I am greatly in earnest in my request. I hope to get Miss —— to give me one. And I will take liberties with both. You must not praise much, promise much.——But as it will be said, " preface by a friend," you may say more than it will become the writer of the piece to say——

A charming postscript! But fraught with " some of your odd notions," as you call them. I do love to express myself in your words.

words.----" Delicacy of mind! Give her hand to one man, whilst her heart sighs for another!" ----Dear Miss Mulso---- *You*, of all young ladies! ----I don't know a young lady, I think, more capable, by the help of time, than you, of reasoning yourself out of a love which you should think improperly placed, and into a duty so zealously urged by indulgent friends, and even by a kneeling father, and silently sighing mother, and of overcoming a first passion. I want to have young people think, there is no such mighty business as they are apt to suppose (and so never struggle against a bias) in conquering a first love. If there were, God help ninety out of an hundred, that marry not their first flames!

I indebted to Miss Mulso three letters besides this!----How can it be?----Your welcome return from your dear P——, I know, made me in debt one; which from time to time, notwithstanding your return, I thought of discharging. Pity me, Madam, if there be two. You know my avocations. I lose a very

very great pleasure, when I am prevented from talking with my pen to my dear Miss Mulso, and of the opportunity of assuring her how much I am, and ever will be,

Her truly paternal friend,

S. RICHARDSON.

TO MISS MULSO.

London, October 5, 1752.

AND so, your fears for my hero and one of my heroines being over, you are afraid the other will be dragged to the altar with the Count de B. I believe I shall not quite displease you, my dear Miss Mulso, in the conduct of this part of my story. But I wish you could have allowed that Clementina might have been prevailed on by such motives as piety

piety and duty, and persuadeableness (no bad quality in a woman), to have chearfully obeyed and obliged parents so dear. I knew a lady who was courted six years, and for five and a half of them loved a man *intolerably*, and the more for her parents withstanding him for that five and a half (for till then she cared not at all for him, and made him her jest). Marry him in January, bury him in June following, and in October next to that, marry a second man, though for two months ready to break her heart for the first! Dear Miss Mulso, you don't know what quick work may be made with women's affections, especially when they meet with parental opposition. Why, my dear, some tender-hearted souls make such a rout about first loves, and-so-forth, that could they overcome their first bashfulness, consciousness, or what can I call it? they would presently overcome every thing else.

Well, but, if I knew how, I should rejoice in pleasing you. But here, when one should advise

advise with you about this scene or that scene, you get out of my reach, and I am left to my own poor invention; and that pleases nobody.

"Difference of religion, you say, did not prevent her love." Why, no. She might not doubt, but if she could get over her pride, and the difference that struck her from consideration of inequality of rank, that he might be prevailed on to change his at the long run, though while the reward was distant she had no great room to think he would.

"Not able to subdue her love!" Phantasy! —Don't you know the lady was a little disordered in her mind? Such persons often retain a little of the first leaven, and it will appear on some occasions. I could give you instances of this. And is it such an extraordinary thing, thus inclined, that the noble enthusiast who could refuse the man of her choice, from religious motives, and thereby make love but of second consideration with her, might not be induced to marry a man so unexceptionable as the Count de B. when she found she could not carry her favourite point? Pho, pho, silly girls! I wish you knew them as well as I.

Thank you, my love, for reminding me of the " manner in which a certain person, who, you say, is not used to be severe in his censures, spoke of a certain young lady, who being almost heart-broken for the ingratitude and perfidy of one man, took comfort (I like your expression) in the address of another, and married in a few weeks." Why, ay, so she did, pretty soul! and I think her only difficulty was, which of two new servants the supposed dying young lady would have. She was a dear, pretty, languishing soul, as I saw myself in one instance: running a thorn into her pretty finger, that her not very pretty boyman might, with dainty needle, daintily pull it out. Why, you must know that this young lady's love case was referred by a friend, a dear female friend (for female friends will hold friendships with each other a great while; ay for years, if both continue single), to the
certain

certain person you wot of: that his sage opinion might make the pretty heart, into which the thorn had been transferred from the finger, easy. He gave his opinion, that the soft soul should pull up all her resolution, and let indignation for apparent neglects, and designed slights, take place of love; and this for her own delicacy-sake, for the sake of the honour of her sex, and-so-forth: and comfort was endeavoured to be thrown in, to encourage the magnanimity. But, alas! no comfort could she take: the certain person was not thought well of for his advice; and the poor dear friend apprehended for the life of her love-sick friend.—Never get over it. No, to be sure! Gone to Bristol! almost dying!—But, behold, in a few weeks two new lovers starting up,—in her sickly state (her frame too delicate, her health thought too precarious for a matrimonial engagement, even with the man she loved), she sends one of the gentlemen (so it is said) of an errand, for the approbation of his friends, and mean time marries the other;

other; flies with him to town, to Ireland; such the state of his affairs requiring: and in a twelvemonth producing a precious infant, declares herself the happiest of women. Thank you, Miss Mulso, for reminding me of this glorious instance of a first affection overcome, without the help of religion, or any thing else but mere *natural* goodness. But the first man was not a Sir Charles. Why no; nor was the lady a Clementina or Harriet. But while the flame was bright and shining, think you a Sir Charles, had he applied, would have been able to have circumvented her whey-faced captain? But she was used ungratefully.— True; but she never thought of the magnanimity of renouncing him on religious motives. Had not two men offered for her to choose out of, perhaps she had persevered, sighed on, desponded, and been a martyr to constancy in love; and every kind heart of the sex, who had known the story, would have had a sigh for Miss B. and a curse for her perfidious *love-yer.*

But

But how, my dear, did the certain person express himself in Miss B.'s case? Did he not triumph, that that delicate young lady had afforded him an instance of his favourite observation in behalf of the vincibility of a first love? Say what you will, my dear Miss Mulso, but every girl that stares abroad at a particular object is not in love.

I myself, indeed, seeing a great deal of delicacy in the frame, in the temper of Miss B., thought she had whined herself into the foible; for the man was not any thing extraordinary, either in person or understanding. But see the proof. And all that have seen the comforter (to speak in your strain) say, Why, truly, Mr. D. is a pretty man; and " O be joyful!—And you have done right; Mrs. L. served the slighter well enough; though you have made him stare, as well as all who thought highly of love, and of your delicacy; for the poor man imagined he had nothing to do but shew his compassion, by breaking off as gently as he could, for fear he should have a life to answer for." Come, come, Madam, raise not such unreasonable expectations on Clementina. Ask Miss H. if she imagined the fair Italian could be more delicate than she thought her fair friend? What a duce, do you think I am writing a Romance? Don't you see that I am copying Nature? Every girl, you will perhaps say, could not do as Miss B. has done. I don't know that. Miss B. would not once have believed this of herself: there may be, as I have hinted, great constancy, great perseverance, if another pretty man offer not while the mind is softened by distress: but if there do — my service to you, Miss B.

Well, but you excuse her, perhaps, by the advice of her physicians at the Hot-Well; by the effect of the Bristol waters drank on the spot. They may be the Lethe of one love, and the inspirer of another. Be it so. In cases of disappointed love, let the girls be packed away to Bristol as fast as they can; and let the pretty gentlemen from Ireland, from Wales, and all the country round, be
admitted

admitted to the salutary springs; and broken hearts will be pieced in less time by many months in a year, than you will allow to poor Clementina for the piecing of hers. So much (and too much, I fear, you'll say) for Miss B. the now exultingly-happy Mrs. L.

My best respects attend your papa, your aunt, and Miss C. I mentioned the last with the honour I have for her to Lady B. This is what that Lady writes upon it:—" The truly learned and excellent Lady, who I was so wicked to hope was not your correspondent, is a prodigy. Learned and a housewife; oftener employed in her domestic duties than with her pen! Pious, benevolent," [an angel!] " modest; as if she knew nothing. This last excellence is the charm of charms."

You wish I could write more frequently. You do me honour in what you say on this subject. And I wish I could hear oftener from my Miss Mulso. Would you so favour me, if *I* wrote oftener? Then you can. Some privileges fathers should have to comfort

fort them in their setting sun. Suppose daughters were not to stand always upon letter for letter? I know your correspondencies engage you greatly. But if you can, were I to write oftener, you can. What is punctilio between father and child, where paternal love is not doubted? I do prodigious things, considering the fire of youth has been long extinguished. Any thing may be done from sixteen to forty.

Every body loves you, and desires cordial respects. I have the happiness to have Mrs. D. at North-End: but am in the circumstances of a miser, who knows that he has a treasure in his chest, and is the easier as he can visit it when opportunity serves. But, ah! the want of that opportunity!

I ever preferred my friend's happiness to my own; I therefore ask not, with the impatience I should otherwise have to see my child, when she returns?

Ever yours, &c.

S. RICHARDSON.

TO MISS MULSO.

August 21, 1754.

WHAT means my beloved child, my ever amiable daughter, by asking " if she may intrude (what a word!) upon me with her pen, after I have declared that I am weary of mine!" ----My quarrel with my pen holds: but there are exceptions: you, my dear, will always be a principal one.

Don't say I was cross to you the last time I saw you. Indeed I was greatly disappointed. I went on purpose to attend you and your papa and aunt----would have no other business. But I believe I was over delicate. I know that even acceptable company, on the eve of a journey, is not always welcome. There is generally too much form for friendship on such occasions. I send up to your good aunt my best wishes and respects, so likely to be well taken. How knew I that your unexpected visitors would

would so soon leave you? But Lady G. and Clementina ran in your head.----There was your regret!

And you have married the latter at last!---- but have not made her very happy.----Happy! child! Who is very happy? Happiness itself is nothing when attained, and happiness is nothing but on comparison; and on reflexion that once we were not so happy. Had we always halcyon days and summer, think you we should be so happy as now, that we have wintery checquerings? Clementina, in the way you have put her, cannot but be happy, having refused, not been compelled to refuse, the man she loved, and having given her hand to a faithful, a virtuous man, who preferred her to all the women in the world.

" Can I forgive my presuming, my tenacious girl?" Why treat you thus freely my amiable daughter? " Yet think not," proceed you, " that I condemn this part of your story." And does my dear Miss Mulso think that, if she had condemned it, I would have

have been displeased with her? Perfection, if attainable, ought not to be aimed at in stories, any more than in characters, designed to display life and manners: the whole piece abounds, and was intended to abound, with situations that should give occasion for debate, or different ways of thinking. And it is but fair that every one should choose his or her party.

What you add on this subject is so much like yourself, that were I to think it necessary to pursue the story, and to imagine that I could to my own satisfaction, I believe, whatever I might have intended, I should be tempted to marry your favourite, and to give your reasons for so doing. Sweet reasoner!— How I love your reasoning pen!—Give me a letter of your Clementina to your other favourite Harriet (you know her inmost soul), as the highest mark of her sisterly confidence, unfolding to her all the emotions of that soul, either on her resolving to comply with the wishes of her friends at the year's end, or on
her

her having for some time past complied with them, and made the Count the happy man you paint him. You know not what use I may make of such a letter. Lady D. has written me one in the character of Charlotte. Your Miss Highmore is inclined to write me one in the character of Harriet. Perhaps, through you, the *meek-eyed Goddess of Wisdom*, our British Minerva, will honour the character of Mrs. Shirley in another; and who knows but, on seeing yours, she will add another in that of Sir Charles, making him shine in some new acts of beneficence? You will flatter yourself, you say, that my pen is at work. It is not;—nor, in my conception, ever can be, but by such inspiration. To me, my imagination seems extinguished.

I have had a fine letter from my new sister, Mrs. Wattes: she is an admirable woman. Her letter glows with true sisterly friendship; but she is at present possessed with too high a notion of her new brother's talents—but will descend, I know, after she has seen by two or three

three letters, that he is inferior greatly to herself. All then I shall hope for is her continued love, though she will see that her opportunities of knowing have been much greater than his; and that he is waning, while she is in full glory. She has given some account of her sweet behaviour to her love-lorn maiden, and to her younger brother, whom she calls Jeronymo. Perhaps it is too tender for the case in all its circumstances. I offered my less tender, but not wholly harsh, assistance for her cure, if she can be brought to have an opinion of me, and if they will appeal to me, as in the case of a third person, as Emily did to Dr. Bartlett—the case of that young lady and the poor Nelly being not wholly dissimilar.

Mrs. D. is returned ill from her romantic excursion. What, what, are the best of you, at any time of life (though you once contended for the independency even of the flirts of your sex in their parents' houses), when you have the misfortune of being freed from controul?

I told

I told Mrs. D. so on this very occasion. But she had a windmill in her head, and away the air of it carried her upwards of one hundred miles from her Doctor; when but a little before, she would not trust herself above three miles from him. Upon my word, Madam, not one good woman in an hundred, is fit to be left to her own head.

Tell your aunt that I greatly revere her.—Angry with her! What an Insolent do you and she suppose me! I should indeed have rejoiced in remembering, that once in the time I have had the honour of knowing her excellent niece, I had been obliged by her visiting my good wife, either in Salisbury-court (she has some city friends, as she passed to them), or at North-End, in her way to Kew. It would have looked, you know, as if we were related by general consent.

Believe me to be

Your truly paternal friend,

S. Richardson.

TO MISS MULSO.

September 24, 1754.

DID I write a letter to my dear Miss Mulso, that was so very grateful to her? When was it? It must have been a great while ago. I remember not any letter lately written by me to her, that deserves so many kind things to be said of its contents. How long have you been at Canterbury, child? I know not but of one letter from you in all the time. If there was any thing extraordinary—why you, my dear, are extraordinary: and it puts me out of conceit with myself, to be applauded for doing but common justice.

"Disputatious girl." Do you call yourself so; or did *I* ever take the liberty so to call you? Because you underscore the word. I love you should differ from me: you give reasons for your differing when you do, which augment my love for you, at least my admiration.

" My disposition of Clementina!" What is that, Madam? Have I in any certain manner disposed of her? I believe not. You give your consent that she shall marry the Count at the year's end. And you give such excellent reasons for her so doing, that if you had written me one of the letters I requested you to write, either on her resolution to marry, or after she had actually given the Count her hand, I might, perhaps, have proceeded.

" Happy, happy." That is such a word with you chits. And do you not own somewhere in the letter before me, that you still love a little romance? But you would have killed Clementina, out of love to her, would you? " Zealous love," indeed!—A lady so qualified to shine! so qualified for an example, in an age that so much wants it!—" Cruel creature," you call yourself: don't expect that I will contradict you. " You believe you have a savage heart," you say. Why, truly.... But, as I said,
I will

I will not contradict you. " Say rather," add you, willing to mend the matter, " thou would'st have consigned her to her kindred angels," &c. &c. Poor matrimony! So the duties well performed of the wifely, the motherly, the matronly character, could not have carried her, divine grace co-operating, to the angelic state. No kindred among them for wives, poor souls!—I am heartily sorry for it!

" Look down (after you had killed her) with pity even on Harriet Grandison."—Charming flight! Her duty on earth unperformed, in the highest characters that a woman can shine in!—O dear! O dear!

" What a proposal!" say you. Why, what a proposal, my dear? Miss C. has refused, you have refused, and been the cause of a more obliging lady's refusal. Well, I can't help it. I was very much in earnest in my request to you all three. Another trial!—I will see, thought I, if they value the poor story so much, as to wish it to be co tinued for one volume more? If they do, surely they

they will contribute each one letter. " You cannot write like Clementina." Have you try'd? You would, on either of the occasions I hinted to you, write better than she. You must needs think—but I will say no more; so flatly denied, and your example so influential. Go, naughty girl, I wish I could avoid loving you. I should not have dared to hope for Miss C. in Sir Charles's character; but that I wanted to make him rise in it, were I to have proceeded. Particularly I wanted a better hymn for him than he had before given us.

" You think you could subscribe to all Mrs. Shirley's sentiments." You rejoice me. But hold. Ah! my Miss Mulso, how could you mock your poor credulous papa? You come with your ifs and your ands. " If I might but be allowed to put in a few queries, and demand a few exceptions and definitions." But what are your queries, &c.? Are there *but* a few of them? I expected to have read them in the next line.

So

So you intended that I should, perhaps, had not your indignation, ill-will rather, to Lady G. come cross you. " You regard her not," you say. " She decides with the presumption of ignorance!" " She never was in love!" What a criterion of judgment you bring, my dear! You write avowedly from your prejudices, to Charlotte's disadvantage. She says very good things (as I have been told); by accident, perhaps. But what then? If they are good things, they will be good things from whatever mouth.

" She has not a heart formed to be in love." Not the unhappier for that. " Not the more amiable for that, in my opinion," say you. May be not in mine. But I am glad that you call passion " a weak excuse for being in love." There's my good girl! Give me your hand. So; we are quite friends again.

" You know she would rank you among the romantic chits." Conscience, child! conscience! I believe she would. " But you care not." Nor I neither. " You don't love her."

her." There are many more that do not; and many more that do. Well, if you don't love her; don't. To be sure, she has great faults. But who shall persuade you to think better of her, when you repeat " I do not, I will not love her. I am angry with you, now you believe." Not I. Nor do you, I suppose, care whether I am or not. You only mention this, for the sake of an angry fling at your poor papa, whom you accuse in so many words, " of having a strange partiality for the rattling creature." Who I, a strange partiality! Well do you add, after saying " that if I am angry, you can't help it (as much as to say you value it not of a farthing), I believe I am very spiteful." Your servant, Madam. The very thing I had said before.

And so Mr. Edward Mulso is still with you —My best respects to him. I know I did not answer a letter of his once written from Kent.

I am glad, so is my wife, to hear from you, Madam, as we were from Miss P., that Miss C. is safely arrived in England. Should young

young people who are so justly beloved, and meet with persons so worthy of their love, be so wholly absorbed as to forget those who brought them acquainted? But perhaps we are more happy in making acquaintance than in keeping lovers. This is our misfortune. But they should " find some honest way," as somebody says, " to acquaint those whom they neglect with their reasons for it."

I wish most ardently that I may always deserve to hold a place in Miss Mulso's affection; and that she will consider me

Her truly paternal friend, &c.

S. RICHARDSON.

TO MISS MULSO.

London, Aug. 15, 1755.

" DIVIDED as I am, between my busy contrivances in town and the happy circle of girls,

girls, have I leisure to think sometimes of my Canterbury girl?—&c." What a question of my dear Miss Mulso! No contrivances, no employment, engagement, or company, can exclude her from my tenderest thoughts for two waking hours together in every revolving twenty-four.

How just are your reflexions on affectation of every sort! But has it been allowed among us (who are us?) that affectation is a necessary piece of decorum? Thank you, my dear Miss Mulso, for telling me of my fault, in being guilty of this fault. I did not know I was. I thought that my native awkwardness might sometimes make me seem guilty, when my heart was tolerably clear of it. Never was there so bashful, so sheepish a creature as was, till advanced years, your paternal friend; and what remained so long in the habit could hardly fail of shewing itself in stiffness and shyness, on particular occasions, where frankness of heart would otherwise have shone forth to the advantage of general character.

racter. But again I thank you, my dear girl, for laying me open to my own observation. Give me the instances, as they recur to your memory, and as they shall occur in future; and I shall love my monitress, and endeavour to amend my fault.

"You suppose I have heard how cruelly you were tantalized by a momentary glimpse of your Miss C." Not I. I was told that you saw that admirable friend at Canterbury; but how short or how long you continued together I knew not. I don't think your P's and your H's are so communicatively filial to me as they used to be: but that may be more my misfortune, perhaps, than their fault. No want of frankness, however, on my side; for though I could be but little with them, I left for their entertainment in my absence many of the instructive letters of my admirable new sister. Come, and live with me, my dear Miss Mulso, on your return, for a month at Parson's-Green; and I will inrich your already rich

rich mind with an intimacy with the heart and powers of this excellent woman.

"Your Highmore has been very good to you, you say----So has your Prescott"----They would not have been good to themselves if they had not. But they could not have the temptations you mention, to divert their attention from you, at Parson's-Green. Very true, my dear. I never knew one of you girls put out of your course, for the pleasure of the poor man whom, nevertheless, you profess to honour. His leisure time is generally in a morning----Did ever any one of you rise an hour sooner in favour to him? You were never visible till the breakfast-table had been spread half an hour----A little arm-in-arm turn in the garden after that was necessary, to relate your dreams, and give account of your night's rest. Change of dress came next----Then dinner-time approached----Then retired to write (till the dinner-bell summoned you) one to one absent favourite, one to another, as love or duty, or both, induced. After dinner

dinner a conversation that could not but be agreeable; but dinner-time conversations are seldom other than occasional prattlings on vague subjects. Attendance of servants will not permit them to be more. Some charming opportunity talked of by-and-by, for reading and conversing. The day we will suppose fine, your Highmore cannot bear to be confined within the house or garden-walls. She throws out her temptations for a walk, where she can see and be seen. All the girls accompany her. ----Nobody must read or be read to, till the walkers return. The man of the house is invited to dangle after them; not for an escorte: they fear nothing. He, aware of his little consequence to them in their walk, stays frequently at home; gives directions to his gardener; and is but just got up stairs to his writing-(I should *now* rather say reading-) desk; when the gipsies' return is signified to him by the call of the tea-bell. Down he must go; for why? They are at *leisure* to expect him. Down goes the passive; finds them, either tired with their walk,

walk, or discontented with the want of variety in the neighbouring fields or lanes. He has the mortification of hearing other situations preferred to his. Poor man! He praised not his situation ; in his heart wished it better for their sakes. Fresh promises to themselves of reading-time. The honest man, who is to be taken up and laid down, as they please, is asked, if he will not read to them by-and-by? He passively bows; the rather signifies compliance, as the opportunity for the book, and his employment, is yet at distance. At last, however (the tea offices all over), they assemble at one large table: one goes to ruffle-making; one to border-making ; one to muslin-flowering ; one to drawing ; and then the passive man is called to his lesson. He is often interrupted by supper-preparations.----At last the cloth is laid ; all the important works bagged up ; each lady looks pleased and satisfied with her part so well performed of the duty of the day : supper, as paradeful a one as if it were a less frugal meal than it always is at Parson's-Green, enters. The business

business of the day is concluded: but *one* difficulty in the whole day; a double one, however----As loth to retire to rest as they are to get together in the morning; and the former perhaps the cause of the latter. Thus concludes the female day among the best of the sex. And a well-passed day too: since, if no great good has been done in it, there has not been much mischief—though some execution might have been aimed at, by some of the rogues who love not to be immured.

> The next is passed as the foregoing day,
> And thus the Summer visit slides away.

Can you read what I have written? O this shaking hand! "No great matter if I cannot" —True, my Miss Mulso. But you must not be sullen, child.—Losers should have leave to speak.

"My spy-window"—Ay, that is the window of vexation—Workmen are----Workmen----I will say no worse of them just now----Only, that

that workmen I wish they were----Yes, yes, yes, yes! I can leave them to their own devices at a moment's bidding, I warrant! and post away to Parson's-Green, when there is a peculiarity, arising from the nature of the business, and the situation to which I am confined, that must be attended to! I am not a woman, child. I do not think the whole world made for me: and I have no mind, were I to fly to Parson's-Green, to find the men employment on my return, by altering what they had done in my absence. Besides, a considerate man would not choose to carry his vexations with him to the place of his recess, and make those he loves partakers of them.

Yet, now I think of it, I might be pretty safe in the latter case. Every one feels not alike. I was preaching to my master-builders very gravely, to confine themselves within the compass of 500l. which they had supposed the erection would cost me. A wise and discreet friend, who had an exceeding good opinion of his own judgment, told them, that it was impossible

possible for them to perform the whole under a thousand.—Last time my good wife was in town, I sent for the master-carpenter to find fault with his slowness, the bricklayers standing still for him. He came while we were sitting lovingly at supper. My wife had a little before peeped at the work from my spy-window; she told him she had. I was just forming my features into a complaining air. Don't you think, Madam, said the sly thief, that we make a great show for the time? [He had just got up a range of window-frames, of eighty foot long, that ought to have been up ten days before] Indeed you do, Mr. Burnell, answered, promptly, the good woman. I did not expect to see the building so much advanced.—I was forced to pull in my horns, as the saying is. The charge of unreasonableness seemed to be implied on the husband, who knew something of the matter; and the wife, who knew nothing at all of it, went off, at her honest man's expense, with the character of a very reasonable, courteous, good sort of a woman.

You bid me " write a few lines to you, if but a few—" Impossible, you see, to write but a few when I write to Miss Mulso—" to tell you how I do." See my trembling hand!----" What I do." I have been writing out anew my books of account, an arduous, an irksome task! The old ones almost written out; for the ease of my kinsman, my own ease, as he is now my overseer; and for the ease of my executors, and justice to my family. These accounts and my building have given me very little opportunity to what I hope I shall have, if it please God to spare me a little longer to such of my friends as are so kind as to wish it, of visiting Parson's-Green for more than one day and night in a week. No great loss, as you will recollect from what I have written in the opposite page; a Miss only when, now-and-then, either accident or occasion reminds them of me.

" But, above all, tell you of your good mamma"----Dearly does she love Miss Mulso, and, allow me to think, well does she deserve th love of all her girls. Nancy loves you, I believe.

lieve, as well as ever, but I hope not more romantically. " I chide her out of it!" Strange if I attempted to do so, I who have thought it not unhappy, that the object chanced to be female that engaged her heart; since girls, at a certain time of life, must be in love with somebody, or something.

You make me vain, when you ask me, if I continue to honour and delight my girl with my paternal love? I am honoured and delighted with the grateful, the kind, recognition from my dear Miss Mulso. In this believe,

My good child,

Your ever affectionate

S. Richardson.

TO MISS MULSO.

London, August 30, 1756.

MY dear and good Miss Mulso, I, too, have been labouring under an increase of my nervous maladies; and these aggravated by a threatening indisposition of my good wife. She is, we hope, in a way of recovery; but, as yet, extremely weak. Your kind letter was brought to me yesterday at Parson's-Green. I read it to her, at her request, as I sat on her bedside. You know how much she loves you. She would make me read on, when I had begun. Was joyful, that you were in an hopeful way; prayed for you; and desired her blessing and best wishes to be conveyed to you----Don't you think, my dear, that between Kew, Sunbury, and Parson's Green, you may recover that health which the Kentish air has not been favourable to you in?

Most

Most heartily do I regret that you saw not Mrs. Wattes: I give her the first place among the women I have the honour to be acquainted with----Don't you be surprised now----I have no doubt but were the others to be tried they would be equally good. But Mrs. Wattes has been cast into the furnace of affliction, and continues to be variously tried; and always comes out pure gold; and still more and more pure. She was greatly disappointed in not seeing Miss Mulso, whom she never saw, but much admires; and Miss Prescott, whom she had once seen, and of whom she retained the most favourable impressions. I rejoice that I lost not one hour of her company in the four or five days I was allowed to enjoy of it. My wife is in love with her. Now, said she, that I have seen Mrs. Wattes I can part with my Nancy to her!

Nancy is accordingly gone from us. Her only concern was her mamma's illness when she set out. The little parting customaries are not to be mentioned. The first ten miles on a journey

journey to a desirable place dissipate all such with the traveller; and the first letter of safe arrival, and so forth, makes the persons deserted, easy.

Don't encourage yourself, my dear Miss Mulso, in an indolence to the pen. If I may judge by myself, an inclination given up of that nature, is not, at will, to be recalled. How irksome to me now is the thought, the obligation of writing! I said, on finishing Grandison (ashamed, and tired, at the thought of the many volumes I had scribbled), that I would write no more for the public; but confine myself to the favours of my correspondents. Stupidity, even to dozingness, has seized me; and, let me tell you, that they are not many with whom I wish to correspond: yet, at the same time, I regret, as I ought, the painful indifference; and the more, as no eligible engagement offers in its place; and I am nothing but supineness and wearisomeness. I have so much grace left me, however, as to be quite out of conceit

ceit with myself upon it. But the evil day seems to be come with me: I have lived much longer than, for many years past, I had reason to expect, from the infirmities I have contended with. I have many warnings. God grant that I may not make them vain!

But with my dear Miss Mulso the case is different. She has youth and genius with her. Yet she must not hurt her health by writing; though she writes with an ease that very few of either sex can equal, as well as with a strength that still fewer can surpass. My dear child, after the kind, the welcome assurances you give me in the sweet letter before me, of the continuance of your filial love, I will not doubt of it. Three lines only, to tell me that you improve in your health, shall always excuse you to me.

You hint that Miss Prescott has brought herself to dislike her pen. She is very ungrateful to it, if so. But the Circuiteer, the beloved Circuiteer, I presume, employs it pretty fully.
I wish

I wish she had a juster opinion, than she has, of her writing powers.

Conclude me, my dear Miss Mulso,

Yours, &c.

S. RICHARDSON.

London, August 2, 1757.

A LETTER from my dear Miss Mulso—I rejoice to see it. Patty, I hope I shan't want your assistance, child. I have written lately (thank God for enabling me!) to three or four of my select friends; and shall I not take up the pen in answer to a letter of Miss Mulso?

I have left off physic. Good Dr. Heberden, in the presence of Mr. John Duncombe, told me that I must not expect relief from it: and I am got deep into tar-water—three or four times a-day, by entreaty of an experienced though

though not medical, friend. I am sure I have better spirits for it; and, do you see else! can hold a pen pretty tolerably. But as to quite recovered, that never can be. I must expect plunges, till the last plunge will set me free.

Yes, my dear, I begin to think Polly is pretty near changing her name. I want to tell you all how and about it, as Lady G. says. There can be no secrets with sisters, and in the same family; can there? Be the matter a little further advanced, and Patty shall acquaint her beloved sister with it all. But a wonderful thing I have to tell you, the girl is to be removed a hundred miles off; and yet the mother is prepossessed in favour of the proposal (rather more, let me own, than the father, though he *dis*likes not). Ah, my Miss Mulso, you know I was always a meek husband; but now I am quite a tame one. But you remember our doctrine—" Parental duty, filial authority! The girl is grown up." And is it not, moreover, very kind in my wife, to
be

be both father and mother to her, in the evil day that has overtaken me? But after all, May the dear creature be but as happy as she will deserve to be from her man! that is all I ask. I have written a great deal: intend to write a good deal more. Were we face to face, I would lay all before you, my daughter, my friend!

Miss C's brother, her pupil, ill in an alarming way! These, my dear, are alarming words. Set my heart at ease about him.

Shame on the men of Kent! Stupid county, indeed! My indignation—But I will say no more—Only shame on the men of Kent, and women too! if the promoting of Miss C's. List of Subscribers is not made a county cause.

I am delighted with what you tell me of young Mr. Duncombe: I have a true esteem for him, and a love of his amiable qualities. What joy to his open-hearted father! Long may they be of comfort to each other! How should I be pleased with the opportunities of hearing

hearing read and preach a certain gent. at Sunbury : and this our other friend at Canterbury!

Reading well you think a more uncommon excellence than preaching well. Very truly, my dear Miss Mulso. Why has it not entered into the heart of some worthy benefactor, as there are professorships of Greek and different sciences, to establish one in each University for lectures in the mother tongue? What have not the French done for theirs, a much less significant one, within the past century?

" You will not enlarge into a tedious epistle." Why not enlarge? Tedious, Madam! Don't affront yourself: but if you will do so, pray affront not me. Whenever you are disposed to favour me, I beg you will enlarge; and not confine your kind intentions to a cardlike compass.

If you have not yourself so good health as you had in London, tell your good aunt that
she

she must, for this one fragment of a summer, deny herself, and send you up to town.

Poor Nancy! She does love you; she is still with Dr. Young: he is kindly fond of her. A seasonable fondness, after what she suffered in the losing of the truly excellent Mrs. Wattes; and, let me say, from the apprehended indifference (lovers you know are always apprehensive) of the worthy object of her love. Poor thing! she knew not that what she attributed to coyness was the effect of prudence in that beloved object; discouraging the aspirations of a young passion, which, at a certain age, intoxicates all the sweet romancers. The old leaven, Miss Mulso. But I am, and ever will be,

Yours, &c.

S. Richardson.

CORRESPONDENCE

BETWEEN

MR. RICHARDSON

AND

MISS S. WESTCOMB.

TO MISS WESTCOMB.

March 6, 1746-7.

How you oppress me, my dear, my ever-amiable and ever-grateful daughter, with the too great value which you set upon what would be indeed trifles, but for the weight and importance given to them by your manners and your kind acceptation! And when you acquaint me that they have been able to alleviate the pangs caused by that cruel attendant, which is so great a drawback upon the comforts

forts of your whole family—what an overpayment is this! And take care, take care, my dear, that you make me not vain, with ten times the reason that you can have to be apprehensive of it.

And could I not, ought I not, unless I had a very great share of vanity indeed, to be diffident of the acceptableness of the truly charming relationship which you honoured me with to your good mamma, till her goodness, in so kind and distinguishing a manner, confirmed it? There can be no merit without diffidence; and I was going to say (if it were not to do dishonour to distinctions which it shall be my endeavour to deserve) diffidence is all the merit I have. I have more friends than my dear L. who think more highly of me than I deserve: and I always endeavour, when I meet with their kind praises, though I doubt not their sincerity, to middle the matter between that and their partiality; and so am guarded against growing vain by the effects of their goodness.

You

You give me pleasure in letting me know, that my proposal to meet your favour and your mamma's, on some airing at North-End, perhaps with Miss Betsey, was not disagreeable. I think, when one's mind can follow one's friends in their retirements, by knowing the places they retire to—as I have seen your charming situation at Enfield; though mine is so inferior that I offer not at comparisons—it affords a good deal of pleasure to a contemplative spirit. Now in your parlour—now in your summer-house—now on one of your walks—now by the side, perhaps angling, as the season invites, of your truly serpentine river; one accompanies a valued friend every where; and to this hour I enjoy the visit I made there—Your mamma, your Anna, your obliging Miss Betsey, in different agreeable attitudes before me; and how nakedly I came home, stript of such agreeable society, by myself, in your Anna's vehicle; and yet I was not always alone as I returned. Some favourable opportunity

tunity may possibly offer, that, though I cannot afford your good mamma and you like happy reflexions, will give me the pleasure afterwards of contemplating, that here—and here—and here—at such a time, I had the company of such and such a respectable friend. You see how selfish I am! But how can I suppose that ye can have equal pleasure in my conversation to what I have in yours?

I cannot help expressing my concern again, that your Mamma's cruel enemy, and as I fear yours, has made a new attack. Perhaps this fit was forming and had got too much head before the tar-water was taken: nay, possibly, the tar-water might, endeavouring to conquer, accelerate it. Methinks it were pity to discontinue it: I have heard of great good from it in the gout, by perseverance. But a distemper so rooted will not easily give way. Yet I dare not advise in a case where a health so important is concerned: yet friendship, and love, and respect, make every body a doctor,
and

and look about, and recollect, and wish to help a suffering friend.

True love is very sensible of slight. Your Anna, I find, thinks a little unkindly of your silence. I will, when I have the pleasure of seeing my dear niece, make your too just apologies known to her: the rather, as I can convey a little reproof with them to herself, who is so backward with her own pen.

I am so extremely hurried in business, that I have had but little opportunity to pay my respects in Tokenhouse-Yard. I am at this time waited for: but wait should every thing, and every body, that would not be detrimented by waiting, challenged as I am, and honoured in the challenge, for a letter as long as your own. You command me to tell the words against yours; I will by-and-by.

And now, my dear, permit me to conclude,
Your most affectionate
and obliged servant,
S. Richardson.

TO MISS WESTCOMB.

WHAT charming advantages, what high delights, my dear, good, and condescending Miss Westcomb, flow from the familiar correspondences of friendly and undesigning hearts!---- Surprising! that the generality of young ladies, delicate by sex, by education; and polite as delicate; their imaginations likewise so happily qualifying them for these mental employments, should be so little sensible of them as they are! ----When styles differ, too, as much as faces, and are indicative, generally beyond the power of disguise, of the mind of the writer!----Who would not choose, when necessary absence, when the demands of an indulgent parent, deprive her of the person of her charming friend, to have a delight in retiring to her closet, and there, by pen and ink, continue, and, as I may say, perpetuate, the ever agreeable and innocent

cent pleasures that flow from social love, from hearts united by the same laudable ties?

I make no scruple to aver, that a correspondence by letters, written on occasions of necessary absence, and which leaves a higher joy still in hope, which presence takes away, gives the most desirable opportunities of displaying the force of friendship, that can be wished for by a friendly heart. This correspondence is, indeed, the cement of friendship: it is friendship avowed under hand and seal: friendship upon bond, as I may say: more pure, yet more ardent, and less broken in upon, than personal conversation can be even amongst the most pure, because of the deliberation it allows, from the very preparation to, and action of writing.

A proof of this appears in the letter before me!----Every line of it flowing with that artless freedom, that noble consciousness of honourable meaning, which shine in every feature, in every sentiment, in every expression of the fair writer!

While I read it, I have you before me in person: I converse with you, and your dear Anna, as arm-in-arm you traverse the happy terrace: kept myself at humble distance, more by my own true respect for you both, than by your swimming robes: I would say hoops, but that I love not the mechanic word!---I see you, I sit with you, I talk with you, I read to you, I stop to hear your sentiments, in the summer-house: your smiling obligingness, your polite and easy expression, even your undue diffidence, are all in my eye and my ear as I read.----Who then shall decline the converse of the pen? The pen that makes distance, presence; and brings back to sweet remembrance all the delights of presence; which makes even presence but body, while absence becomes the soul; and leaves no room for the intrusion of breakfast-calls, or dinner or supper direction, which often broke in upon us.

Not that these cares, neither, are to be neglected; nor, indeed, any of the least duties of that

that œconomy which falls properly under a
lady's inspection: I have taken care to make
my Clarissa, whom you obligingly three times
in your letter take notice of, inculcate this doc
trine,—that all the intellectual pleasures a lady
can give herself, not neglecting the necessary
employments that shall make her shine in her
domestic duties, should be given; but otherwise that she should prefer the useful to all
theoretic knowledge. But this is one of the
felicities that give a preference to familiar cor-
respondencies---that they may be carried on,
and best carried on, at the retired hour, either
morning or evening, before needful avocations
take place, or after they have been answered.
For the pen is jealous of company. It ex-
pects, as I may say, to engross the writer's
whole self; every body allows the writer to
withdraw : it disdains company; and will have
the entire attention.

Writing to your own sex I would principally
recommend; since ours is hardly ever void of
design,

design, and makes a correspondence dangerous:---Except protected by time, as in my case, by general character, by choice already filled up; where is the man that deserves to be favoured?---And were there the least room to suspect that there was any thing less than paternal in my views, I would not dare to urge the favour, or take the liberty.

But it is the diffidence I wish to banish: the diffidence! which, in the right place, is so great a beauty in the charming sex;---- but why the diffidence to such a one as I am! ----a plain writer: a sincere well-wisher: an undesigning scribbler; who admire none but the natural and easy beauties of the pen: no carper: and one who has so just an opinion of the sex, that he knows, in an hundred instances, that the ladies who love the pen are qualified by genius and imagination to excell in the beauties of this sort of writing :----and that bashfulness, or diffidence of a person's own merits, are but other words for undoubted worthiness;
and

and that such a lady cannot set pen to paper but a beauty must follow it; yet herself the last person that knows it.

But do not, dear Madam, in the future favours you bid me hope for, make apologies for length. The person who sits down, designing brevity, writing to a friend, on subjects of conversation and friendship, hastening, as I have known some visibly do, in their first line to the last, must, if leisure allow a larger letter, intend a slight. For what friendly heart can want a subject on such an occasion; when it must be sensible, that the goings out, the comings-in, the visit either meditated, paid, or received, the visitors, the reading or musical subjects, the morning meditation, the mid-day bower, the evening walk: what she hopes, what she wishes, what she fears, are proper topics for the pen; and what friendship cannot be indifferent to. For what one thing is there, that a friend does, or is concerned in, or for, which can be too slight a subject to a friend?

I am, dear Miss Westcomb,
>Your most obliged correspondent,
>>S. RICHARDSON.

TO MISS WESTCOMB.

WHAT names, my dear and too diffident correspondent, do you call yourself?—Do you think I will allow of the liberties you take with the gentlest, sweetest-tempered person in the world? Is there not a justice due to one's self, as well as to the rest of the world? No fear, my dear, in such an ingenuous mind as yours, that any thing but emulation can follow deserved praise: and how noble a grace is emulation!——May none of my daughters, by nature, ever be in more danger in this respect, than the daughter of my heart! and then I am sure they never will be vain hussies.

But now I have named North-End, what shall we say to your beloved Anna? She has indeed done me the honour of a letter of ten or twelve lines, highly excusable that it was no longer, being the product of a sudden impulse,

pulse, and at twelve at night. But having broke the ice I had hopes she would have made the less scruple to proceed; and especially when she mentioned her hopes of a letter from me to Kent, whither her papa and she went soon after; which letter I wrote. Yet cannot I prevail upon her to second her favour. Now, I must own that diffidence of one's own abilities, in man or woman, is not only a rare (such is the age we live in!) but a very commendable quality; so commendable, that I believe there is hardly any thing well done, well said, or well written, but by persons who have a competent share of it. Fear of not doing well always manifests a desire to do well: and what difficulty can be conquered without an ardour to conquer?---Those who have no doubt must be ignorant: they have nothing to be informed of; at least they think so themselves; while every one else sees they know nothing, and are not in the way to know any thing that shall give them distinction or excellence;----while the modest or diffident person wants

wants but to have her bosom unlocked, as I may say, or her lips opened, by conscious yet not gross praises, and she will surprise herself into sentiments that she knew not she had in such perfection, and delight every body to whom she communicates them. Tell the dear Anna, and be pleased yourself, my dear, to know, that the pen is almost the only means a very modest and diffident lady (who in company will not attempt to glare) has to shew herself, and prove that she has a *mind*. Set any of the gay flutterers and prattlers of the tea-table to write---I beseech you, set them to write---and what will they demonstrate, but that they can do nothing but prate away?--- And shall the modest lady have nothing but her silence to commend her? Silence indeed to me is a commendation, when worthy subjects offer not, and nothing but goose-like gabble is going forward; for air and attention will shew meaning, beyond what words can, to the observing: but the pen will shew soul and meaning too.---Retired, the modest lady, happy

happy in herself; happy in the choice she makes of the dear correspondent of her own sex (for ours are too generally designers), uninterupted, her closet her paradise, her company herself, and ideally the beloved Absent; there she can distinguish herself: by this means she can assert and vindicate her claim to sense and meaning.—And shall a modest lady then refuse to write? Shall a virtuous and innocent heart be afraid of leaving its impulses embodied, as I may say?—Shall she refuse to give herself, by use, a facility in so commendable an employment; which on many occasions may be no less useful than commendable?—Shall she deny herself a style; and, as I may say, an ability to judge of the style or sense of others, or even of what she reads?—Hard, very hard, would she think it, if our sex were to make a law to deny her the opportunities she denies herself! When you have the pleasure of each other's company, pray revolve these things, and give force to them, for the subject is pregnant by your own reasonings.

But

But the difficulty will be in the choice of the correspondent. If of our sex, an artful, a designing, an indelicate heart endeavour to obtrude itself upon hearts so diffident, so modest, so worthy: if a person be capable of endeavouring to warp such worthy hearts from their duty, to insinuate himself in such a manner as to give room for suspicion, that he would induce, or lead, their choice, in the grand article of life: if he be not guarded by years, by the character long held of a warm and friendly heart, delighting to encourage the youth, especially of the gentler sex, in pursuing the laudable examples and courses of the families they are sprung from; then let him be shunned, avoided, and treated with contempt.

I am extremely obliged to your honoured mamma for her favourable notice and approbation of a correspondence, that would have been censurably begun without her leave, had it not carried unexceptionableness in the very face of it. If it had not, I am sure her beloved and dutiful daughter would not have given it the least countenance; nor would the worthy

worthy and prudent, and equally dutiful Anna have given it her sanction, though she is so loth to contribute to it by her pen. I beg my most respectful compliments to the good lady. I hope her journey has given her health; and then you must both have had high delight in each other. For, my dear, a wise and indulgent parent, and a child grateful and sensible of that indulgence, must give hourly pleasures to each other: pleasures, if possible, more poignant and exalted than those of friendship, exalted as those are; since friendship is included in such a harmony: reverence on one side can be no impediment, because paternal or maternal love and condescension require nothing of that but what is equally reputable to both to be shown.

Adieu, my dear, and be happy! Rowe justly says,
—————— To be good, is to be happy:—Angels
Are happier than men, because they're better.

If there were sex in heaven, good women would be angels there as they are here.

Your paternal and faithful friend,
S. Richardson.

TO MR. RICHARDSON.

Enfield, June 27, 1750.

DUTY and gratitude both call on me to write to my dear papa; being now, through the favour of God, recovered from my indisposition, and again permitted to say (what I have said a hundred times before, but never can too often repeat) that I think myself too much honoured by your favour, and the kind concern your humanity and goodness made you feel for us invalids, not to acknowledge it as early as possible, in the most grateful terms.

Indeed we have had a sad sick-house, or rather hospital: for after my mamma, Betsey, and myself, got somewhat better, one of our maid-servants fell so dangerously ill with the same complaint, that her life was despaired of.

I am sorry for the uneasiness you have been under for us, and the disagreeable time you had

had here; indeed it was then a very sad one to you. Suppose, good Sir (for after what has passed I am afraid of downright asking it; nay, though I could claim a promise; so suppose I say), that you should again oblige us in the same way with a visit?

So think of it; and I assure you, as far as our capacity permits, we will endeavour as an amends to make it more tolerable: for no summer-house shall be locked, &c.

I must own self-interest prompts me to make this request. And though I love to be excited by more generous motives, I think herein I am excusable, as your conversation is equally improving and delightful; so that, if I have not bettered, from frequently enjoying this happy advantage, I can attribute it only to myself, in not having a memory to retain, and a genius to improve by it; but what I can, I will. So, dear Sir, be not wanting on your part; for much I have to learn.

My dear mother, whose life is most precious to me, I have the grief to see daily declining, and

and visibly drawing nearer and nearer to that awful period the youngest must, ere long, experience. She tells me, on observing my distress for her (and with tears I write it), I depress my spirits too much; that it is a duty we owe to God and ourselves, not to repine at the dispensations of the All-wise Being and Supreme Director of events; nor by an immoderate concern to destroy health and perhaps life. But, alas! of what comfort are these remonstrances? Do they not serve to endear her more to me, and render me very reluctant to the thoughts of such a separation? Hard trial! And how is the loss of so invaluable a parent, friend, and adviser, to be supported, in whom is comprised all my earthly felicity? For her conversation is my entertainment; her lessons my instruction; and her affection my pride and joy. How far then her persuasions are from producing the desired effect, I leave any one to judge.

I told you, my dear papa and second parent, this would be a dull, serious, perhaps stupid letter:

letter: for what prospects have I? How uncheerful to look forwards!

But I ought not to anticipate what may happen; for at that rate we should never enjoy any blessing, from the certainty of there coming a time when we shall be deprived of them.

You see how melancholy a time I have; made so on this account, and not from the retirement I am in; for that to me is rather agreeable, not being of a very gay disposition: for between reading, working, music, writing, and other in-door amusements, and walking, fishing, &c. without, I am so well entertained, that if it were not for the allay I mention, I should possess a perfect tranquillity and should know my own happiness too well to envy the gay inhabitants, as I may call them, of Ranelagh's lofty dome, or Vauxhall's rural scenes. Not that I would have it thought I am such a recluse, that, if I were in the way of these places, I should never frequent them, though I would not dwell in them. Far otherwise:

otherwise: you know me better than to suppose it; and have been so indulgent to me, as not to condemn my sometimes attending public places in moderation.

Alas! good Sir, how often is that? Sure that word, with its near neighbour, viz. *innocent pleasures,* is sadly perverted, or I have greatly misunderstood them; for according to that, if I were willing to take advantage of it, they seem, in the light the world takes them, to be very extensive; since they judge of them by no other standard than their own inclinations; and those often allow them to go a great way. But I shall be very glad of your sense of the words for my direction, and shall esteem myself very happy to be made acquainted with them.

I doubt you have been, in all respects, too soft with me. For am I to think 'tis from any mark of your regard you are so tender? Ought I not rather to fear it proceeds from indifference? For have you not said that those

those you love most, you never fail, on occasion, to reprove? I should therefore wish, yet dread, to be by you on the perusal of this trash, to hear your ingenuous reflections on it, and then see you commit it to the flames, that it might no more appear against me.

But now for your comfort, and to let you see that the longest letter has an end, I will not add more, than that I am, with filial affection, dearest Sir,

Your daughter, sincere friend,

and obliged servant,

SAR. WESTCOMB.

TO MISS WESTCOMB.

London, July 2, 1750.

HOW sweetly, my dear Miss Westcomb, do you affect and grieve me, by the charming expression

expression of your concern, so truly filial, so worthy of my Miss Westcomb, for the indisposition of your dear and good mamma! But the Almighty will, I hope, continue to you the blessing you are so laudably earnest to have continued to you for many happy years. Disorders have been out-lived. May hers be so! She has great, and I had almost said, counterbalancing comforts, in the duty of such a daughter. Sore throats may affect temporarily; gouts may torture—but the limbs, the body only can they torture. An undutiful child can break the heart-strings asunder—can tear the mind in pieces: while a dutiful one strengthens the heart of the indulgent and grateful parent.

How happy, in this capital instance, are you all! The heart, my dear, must be whole and often gladsome, contemplating on such filial blessings. Shall we not then hope for continued life, if not complete health, to such an happy parent?

Yet with your cares you must continue your fears.

fears. The deprivation would be irreparable. You must have anxieties. But let them not be such as shall dishearten, or wound the peace (the only way you can wound it) of that mind which you are so dutifully desirous to preserve. Her grief, her tenderness, must be augmented by yours. Turn always to her the sun-shine of hope, and remind her of past sufferings nobly supported in the course of a long illness; and this will irradiate her mind, rather than add to her hopelessness of amendment. Once or twice I observed, when I had the pleasure to be with you last, that your sincere grief for your mamma's sufferings (and exquisite they seemed to be) made you acknowledge the justness of her apprehensiveness, and of your own fears. Your eyes most charmingly acknowledged it as well as your lips. I would wish you to appear touched, sensibly touched. You ought, and you cannot help it. But throw in always, my dear child, the balm of Hope: " And come, my dearest mamma, my love, my soul, my joy," (and all the tender

der words you so beautifully are accustomed to apply to her) " you have been worse----at such a time----and at such a time, you remember. And God, I hope, will be your comfort, and my comfort. Is it not in Him alone that we trust? And how many blessings have we with our afflictions, that other people have not in as great? Come, my dear mamma, let us hope! Be comforted! Have you not in me, daughter, husband, friend, lover? Is not our Betsey good, dutiful, obliging? Have we not many friends?---Come, my dear mamma, let us hope----God, who has so often delivered you and preserved you against probability, is still at hand—his power and his goodness unabated----We will hope!"

Excuse me, my dear Miss Westcomb, for presuming to put words in the mouth of a young lady, who could write as follows, and whose words only I needed to have repeated: "But I ought not to anticipate what may happen; since, were we to give ourselves anguish, in apprehension that a time will come when we shall be be deprived of what we most value, we should never be able to enjoy the blessings we have in possession."

You have so many natural beauties in your own situation; such a fine piece of water, naturally serpentine; such extended and noble prospects, that I wonder the less that you can sit down satisfied without letting your thoughts rove to Vauxhall and Ranelagh. What advantage has either of those places, but in the gay multitude, over your more truly rural scenes?

What must the minds of those persons be, who can wish to live in a crowd?

Every season to see and be seen at such places once, twice, thrice, to such ladies as you, who can appear with advantage any where, must be agreeable, must be justifiable, and even oftener to oblige friends; and when parties are made, which youth and condition of life ought not to make you decline. But to frequent them, in the proper sense of the word, is to make by degrees the duties of life and the domestic pleasures, pains, and irksome. It is to live for the eye and the ear only: it is to make one in a crowd, an unheeded crowd, because a crowd; and to render cheap that person, that face, that sweetness of mien and aspect, that dove-like amiableness, which seldomer seen would attract; and be rather spoken of for discretion in absence, than distinguished by often repeated presence, if I may so say.

From what I have said, you will gather, Madam, what notion I have of the words moderation and innocent pleasures. Those pleasures must be always innocent, that innocently amuse; and which divert not the mind from its domestic and superior duties, but serve as whets or sharpeners to duty, by a well-judged variety and change of scene. But when the love of out-door pleasures makes the in-door duties pall; and when it becomes irksome to be at home; and the mind hankers after opportunities of looking out of itself, then are such amusements dangerous: then cease they

they to be innocent. Then will they exceed, in all probability, the bounds of moderation.

But as to the word moderation, many persons deceive themselves in the application of it to themselves, by looking forward to those who are immoderately fond of public appearance, and, as you well express it, dwell on the gay spots. " Such a lady and such a lady are never absent. But I—don't go above once a week to Vauxhall"—[the weather not always favours]—" and not above twice a week to Ranelagh. In the winter, not above three or four times a week to plays, concerts, operas—which Lady Such-a-one never fails to be at, one or other, every night. I am therefore moderate."

But we should never justify ourselves by the examples of the gay. There is a right and a wrong. A prudent lady will endeavour to distinguish the boundaries of both, and will profit by the examples of the best, rather than justify herself by the liberties of the worst— A poor boast for a worthy mind to male

" 'Tis true, I may a little exceed----but I am not so faulty as some whom we all know."

But what a glorious part have you chosen! (the better part indeed!) who can say, " That you could delight in your retirement----That you could most agreeably divert yourself by reading, working, music, writing, and other necessary in-door amusements; and with walking, fishing, &c. without-doors, were it not----" For what? Why (excellent!) were it not for the allay given you by the ill-state of health of a dear, an indulgent mother!

Too gentle in blaming you, my Miss Westcomb! You say, " You are afraid that my not blaming you oftener than I do, may probably proceed from my indifference to you, since I have confessed, that I never spare those I love." Dear lady! What can I blame you for? What room for blame do you give me? For praise you do give me room! And I admire and love you for what you have written on this occasion.

Go on, dear Madam, in cherishing, in loving,

ing, in blessing, I may say, that dear parent whose health you so beautifully as well as dutifully acknowledge to be of so much importance to you. You will add to the days as well as to the comfort of her to whom you owe your being, by your assiduities about her. And, when (not till many years I hope are past, and she has seen and rejoiced in your happy settlement in marriage) she shall be called upon to resign to the common lot, how will you be blest in your own reflections, on a duty so well performed! and how will you be entitled to expect a return from yours to you! For no duty is more rewarded in kind, as I have often had opportunity to observe, than the filial.

Here is a long letter, close written, and in a nervous paroxysm, as I may say. Excuse on that account all its imperfections—I cannot transcribe. Let us pray for the health and happiness of each other. I always will for that of your dear mamma, my sister, my friend: for yours, my beloved daughter; and for Miss Betsey's, including that of every one dear to each of you, as becomes

Your truly paternal

and ever-affectionate friend,

and humble servant,

S. RICHARDSON.

Mrs. J. made my wife and me a visit. I told her how much you regretted the coldness, &c. and how much, nevertheless, you valued her. She expressed unabated value for you, and said she had written to you; and excused herself in a very pretty manner, for her only seeming neglect. I was glad she had written, I told her, before my chiding. She said she would get the favour of your company to Ankerwyke. But I must have you all first (must I not?) at North-End.

TO MR. RICHARDSON.

Enfield, July 26, 1750

YOUR last kind favour, my dear sir, and still kinder call, when you hesitated not at putting yourself to an inconvenience to oblige your friends with your company here, deserved my earlier thanks: but I have been prevented writing till now; for my mamma has (through many persuasions that it might be of service to her health, and give some amusement, rather than sitting always in her chamber) sent for a chair from London; in which she is carried every day from eight in the morning till nine at night, excepting meal-times; and as I walk with the chair almost the whole time, I am scarcely ever in the house, and consequently have no opportunity for writing. Indeed, if it did not do good in a material instance, I could be quite displeased with it; for it mis-spends

spends my time most sadly. You may probably say, But what necessity is there for you to walk so much, because your mamma for her health is obliged to ride? Yes, my good sir, there is; namely, that it would be so unsociable for her to be separated from the whole family, that her little prattler is therefore obliged to accompany her. But rather than suffer longer in your opinion by not writing, I have left this dear mamma in the open field to resume this long-neglected employ; and I hope you will not charge the quitting her to me as a fault, since on another occasion I have known you not to condemn an innocent elopement. It has hitherto not been in my power to accept your most agreeable invitation to North-End; but I hope, and design, before the summer is quite over, to do myself the pleasure to wait on you; for no place shall I think of visiting, till I have paid my duty where I owe it with the utmost gratitude; for the heap of obligations on my side is continually increasing, and
already

already arrived at such a height, that, considering I am but short, I can scarce reach them with a finger, nor yet with my pen.

The celebrated Miss G—ngs have for a while already left Enfield; the place, together with the assembly, not being gay enough to retain them; so are gone in pursuit of more brilliant diversions; and may the Installation, Sunning Hill, &c. do more for them than Enfield could! May toupees, powder, lace, and essence (the composition of the modern pretty fellows) follow them in troops, to stare, and be stared at, till the more bashful youths give the first blush! I cannot suppose you will censure me as either envious or ill-natured, in writing thus freely; since, as to the former (if I were weak enough), they are so far out of the reach of any competition, that it is needless to say any thing in my excuse, self being out of the case; and I likewise think I may be allowed to add, without eating one sour grape with the fox in the fable, that I would not for all their advantages of person change

change conditions: indeed I would not, if it were possible, on any consideration, though at the present I know nothing essentially bad of them, as to fact, but a disposition and situation in life too apt to lead them astray: and for myself, if in this instance (though in no other) I should offer to name myself with them, I can only observe, that notwithstanding I am far, very far, from being what I wish, or any way deserving, yet, having the use of reason to direct which path is best to tread in, there may be hopes of one day arriving at some degree of perfection in a confirmed and steady virtue; when neither temptation shall overcome, afflictions depress, prosperity elate, or disappointments make me despair: but I shall on all occasions behave with a suitable composure and decency, prepared for every trial and event. But I ask pardon for thus running on; my best and good papa will excuse me; for is he not ever ready to take the overflowings of my pen and heart? Do I not often unburden myself to him in occasions interesting
indeed

indeed to me? But are they so to any one else? But this friend kindly concerns himself for me, licenses my pen to flow, my heart and tongue to speak; and then comforts and consoles with never-failing tenderness and eloquence. I am, dearest papa,

>Your sincere and unalterably
>
>>affectionate daughter, friend,
>>
>>>and obliged servant,
>>>
>>>>S. WESTCOMB.

TO MISS WESTCOMB.

August 6, 1750.

I REJOICE, my dear Miss Westcomb, that your mamma has fallen upon the method of the London chair. What, as she has servants that can carry her about her own sweet grounds, if she bought one that she might alleviate her gouty tortures, and give herself air, and winter at Enfield, as she has put off her house in town, and is not perhaps provided with another? Let me tell you, that there are as many pleasant winterdays as summer, taking the spangled frosts of the winter against the extreme heat of some of the summer months; and cold is a bracer, as heat, I well know by dear experience, is a relaxer. Consider of it, dear ladies. You may warm in winter, by additional logs or hillets, to what degree you will, but in summer there is danger in cooling.

You make me ask,—" What necessity is there for your walking so much, when your mamma rides?"—Have you not asked me to chide you? You have now given me an opportunity—You are a naughty girl, for what you put in my mouth on this occasion, and for what you, moreover, write upon it, as taking up so much of your time. Can you pass it better, than in accompanying and talking to your mamma all the time? Must it not delight

light you, to observe your mamma's spirits rise, as the scenes, through which she is carried, vary? Why, child, you are the soul of your mamma's comforts. She is the delight of your heart. And can you, let me repeatedly ask, bestow your time better? And will not the walking exercise be a means of confirming your own health? To ride to recover health, and to walk to continue it, is a medical rule. You may angle in your own delightful stream; and your mamma can be carried about you and about you, when you are tired. You may snatch a page or two of reading in your pretty new-built, or your formerly-built summer-house; and you will both meet with a fresh appetite and new subjects for discourse from the momentary absences.—As to writing to me—let that alone, whenever it would interfere with these mother-comforting excursions. A blessing will attend you for it; and great comfort on reflection, if it should please God to take from you that dear parent. Your own children, on
a change

a change of your condition; will bless, and, most probably, follow the example. It is sweetly pretty for mothers to have an opportunity to tell their children how dutiful they were to their mothers; and what pains they delighted to take, to the foregoing all other enjoyments, to preserve their healths, and to continue their lives.

But you are so very good, so laudably dutiful, that I might have spared the greatest part of what I have written. Only to show my dear daughter (in order to give credit to my praises, for which there is, in your whole conduct, so much room) that not a shadow of a fault, though but in words, should escape my observation and animadversion.

I am delighted with all you write in relation to the two Misses G—. These poor girls seem too much in haste to make their fortunes, to catch their fish. When women turn seekers, it will not do. Gudgeons may bite; but not even then but by accident, and through inexperience of the wiles of anglers. Are gudgeons

geons worth their baits?---I hear they have been rudely treated at Windsor, as they were at Edmonton. The poor girls cannot help the rudeness of men. They are to be pitied for it. But when once they are made so cheap, as that all the reverence that beauty should inspire is departed, and they become the subject of affront, they are in danger of being blown upon. Even rakes, who have no delicacy themselves, admire delicacy in women. And when these come to be considered as fortune-hunters of their sex, without a shilling of their own, they will run the fate of fortune-hunters of ours, and that deservedly. What business have these girls to flutter about in high life, when they have not either sense or fortune to become the middling? " *We show-girls,*" said a certain single lady with more good sense than these girls have to boast of, " never get husbands." Another young lady, whom I have the honour to know, has had more overtures made her, though she has not thought fit to accept of any of them, than these

these girls are likely to have, yet never was from under her mother's wing; and, most probably, for that very reason. Men approach not this young lady but with views of strict honour. The two sisters may justly suspect the address of every man who approaches them. They are already considered as the property of public company. Every eye has a right to them.

What is become of the delicacy of the sex, when a fair face, and fine features, without any other merit, shall allowably push girls into public life, and declaredly with a view to captivate---to make prey, I should rather say—of the first man they shall think considerable enough to support them in their glare and vanity?—To my dear Lady B. I have wished them, and that in charity, the small-pox, if they have not had it; and that their faces might be seamed with it: and I have quoted these lines, with which I shall conclude what I have to say of them at present:

Beauty!

Beauty! thou art a fair, but fading flow'r,
The tender prey of ev'ry coming hour.
In youth, thou, comet-like, art gaz'd upon,
But art portentous to thyself alone.
Unpunish'd thou to few wert ever giv'n;
Nor art a blessing, but a mark, from heav'n.

Yours, &c.

S. RICHARDSON.

TO MR. RICHARDSON.

Enfield, Oct. 15, 1750.

THE only reason my dear papa has not yet heard from me is, that I have been returned from Ankerwyke but a few days, my mamma's amended health after my leaving her permitting my long absence; and while from home I had not leisure to write.

The favours I received from yourself, and the worthy Mrs. Richardson, were infinitely obliging;

obliging; but what I esteem equally so, was your kind remembrance of my mamma in the fruit you sent her by the return of our coach; she ate forth your praise in every peach, grape, &c. We have since jointly agreed, that in this, as in all other instances, you are very ingenious in finding out ways to delight, and surprise; for trifles conferred with delicacy are more acceptable than considerable favours ungracefully bestowed.

It was a great concern to me, both to leave North-End so soon, where I thought myself quite happy, and not to have your company down with me; and notwithstanding the difficulties I was under about going, I found the offer of the coach not altogether to my wish, since it straitened me sadly for time, and hurried me away before I otherwise needed.

As to Ankerwyke, it is a most charming place, though I suppose you may partly know it, or have had a description of it; therefore for me me to attempt saying much would be unnecessary.

The fine lawns, winding river, cultivated lands, and, to sum up all in a word, that enchanting spot called Cooper's Hill, in full view of the house, are very delightful without-doors; but it is not more so than the agreeable freedom, cheerful company and conversation of the family within; for they kindly made this place, naturally delightful, still more so by varying our pleasures, every day inventing something new. After breakfast we sometimes rowed up the river for about half a mile; then landed, and walked on to see several of the fine seats, and gardens, with which this country abounds; afterwards walked on over hills and high mountains—nor did bushes or briers deter us—commanding all the way the most beautiful prospects imaginable; at another time went out on a party of fishing, though seldom catched any thing, no, not even a gudgeon: but you know, Sir, I have no luck that way; yet still it was all charming: now and then, for change, took a break.

a breakfast and dance at Sunning-Hill; returned more gay than we went; to which succeeded converse, music, working, reading; and a rubber at whist concluded the night. I ought not to have omitted, many pretty long intervals were filled up with prattling to the little girl; for she is a most engaging, sweet creature.

And now I will submit readily to your decision, whether these were censurable amusements or not; for am I not your daughter, and permitted by adoption to call you father? Therefore is it not consistent with my duty to recount ingenuously all that passes?

This has been, and will ever be, a rule with me in my conduct to my mamma; for, though I sometimes have the mortification of owning disagreeable truths, it is what I cannot dispense with, in order to know better; and sure there is a merit in sincerity, which this alone can be the test of.

I can now no longer forbear saying to my dear papa, that I do not think he did well by
his

his poor girl, in not coming, though but for a day, to Ankerwyke, while I was there, and so fully depended on you; especially when I, out of punctilio, would not go there till after my visit to North-End.

You see how saucy I am in thus making you accountable to me; but as it is not the first instance, by many, that I have given of it, and been forgiven, I presume upon obtaining it now from my dear papa, and am, with all sincerity and regard,

Your very affectionate and obliged

S. WESTCOMB.

TO MISS WESTCOMB.

Nov. 1, 1750.

WAS there ever such a daughter heard of as my Miss Westcomb, to know herself to be in fault;

fault; and yet to take none upon herself, and lay it all upon her papa!

You know, my dear, how ready I held myself to attend you to Ankerwyke: you know what a piece of self-denial I gave myself, and what a regret your mamma Richardson, to consent to part with you, for your own satisfaction and pleasure, days before you would have left us. And, on this occasion, I could almost remind you what a painful child you were to me the Saturday preceding, by your pretty volatility and heedlessness. You know that you would not accept of my conveyance to Ankerwyke; as if the pleasure I should have had in the company of a daughter so dear to me, for eighteen or twenty miles together, was to be given up for the sake of a paltry expense, which you would not have mattered in the like case, though you made it a consideration worth regarding for me.

Well, and after this you could stay at Ankerwyke but a few days truly, and must hasten back to the dearest of mammas! Well, and then,

then, like a good girl, you could send me a
note, and with the voluntary promise of a letter
to follow it. No letter came. Week after
week passed; nothing heard I of my girl. To
be sure, at the beginning of the second week,
thought I, she is gone back to Enfield. At
the beginning of the third week, if she could
not have called upon us, as she went by the
turning that led to the deserted North-End
(two bow-shoots, and no more) in her way to
her best-beloved mamma, she might have written to me, to let me know how and where she
was. Still another week, and another passed—
No daughter to be heard of! No Miss Westcomb! Lord forgive the child! Lord preserve
my girl! thought I: what is become of her?—
Ill, I doubt! Or sent for to Enfield, her mamma ill; and no heart to write—And then I
pitied you all!

But behold! (Some comfort, though slighted!) on the 16th of October in the year of our
Lord one thousand seven hundred and fifty,
comes a letter dated the day before from Enfield,

field, to acquaint me, " that the only reason that a certain person's dear papa (I say, dear papa!) had not heard from her, was, that she was but a few days before returned from Ankerwyke!"—The very reason, in short, that he should have heard from her, and the rather, because she promised by word of mouth, as well as by written note, that he should!—And a further reason urged, that of her mamma's amended health! Astonishing!—Since that happy event should have given her spirits to write, as it would have given me joy to hear the good news.

But I must own, that there were other reasons suggested—And what were they?----Why, " Ankerwyke was a charming, a most charming place. Its fine lawns; the winding river, that runs by it; the cultivated lands, that surround it; the inchanting spot called Cooper's Hill, in full view of the house, without-doors: the agreeable freedom, the chearful company and conversation (Poor North-End!) within; made Ankerwyke (naturally delightful) so much

much more so, by varying your pleasures, by inventing every day something new, that it was impossible to think of the poor papa and mamma, and sister, you had left."

And, indeed, what time had you, were inclination to have offered----since no writing-matters could be performed (unless a violent inclination indeed had impelled!) before breakfast? And after breakfast it was impossible; since then " you sometimes rowed up the river for half a mile; then landed, and walked on to see several of the fine seats and gardens with which that country abounds: afterwards walked on over hills and high mountains (High stiles you mean, Madam!), neither bushes nor briers deterring you (which might make mending-work necessary when returned, perhaps; and so add to your employments), commanding all the way the most beautiful prospects imaginable. At other times going out on a party of fishing, though seldom caught any thing (No, Madam, nor deserved to catch any thing!---- How could you expect luck, when so undutifully

fully forgetful of your promise?)----Yet still, you say, all was charming, catch or not catch!----for now-and-then, for change, you took a breakfast at Sunning-Hill, and a dance too!"---- I heard of you from that place! I did so!---- " Returned more gay (and more forgetful of course!) than you went! (How could either papa or promise be remembered, thus gaily diverted?) Especially when to these amusements, these charming amusements, succeeded converse, music, working, (Did you say working?) reading!---(Ay, reading!)----And a rubber at whist (No questtion!) concluded the night." If my dear girl tells me that she had no time for her prayers, I am sure I ought to forgive her!---But, " besides all these, pretty long intervals were filled up with prattling to the little girl; for she is, say you, a most engaging, sweet creature."

" And now will I submit readily to your decision, say you, as your daughter, whether these were censurable amusements, or not."----Censurable? No, Madam!---They could not be censurable,

censurable, otherwise than as they so wholly engrossed you; that they allowed you no time to discharge a voluntary promise; allowed you no time to let your papa know, that your stay at Ankerwyke might have afforded him more than one offer of attending you and your good friends there; when he was so unhappy as not to be able to go at one time, and prevented, when you know he had designed to go, at another. And pray let me ask you, Madam----When Mrs. Jodrell retired to write to her sister, and Miss Johnson to her papa, what hindered, but want of inclination, that you could not make use of that opportunity, had not any other been afforded you, to write to yours?

Yet, that is the jest of it, to come with your complaint----" I can now no longer forbear saying to my dear papa (Yes, dear papa, when I have leisure to think of him), that I don't think he did well by his poor girl, in not coming, though but for a day, to Ankerwyke, when I was there, and so fully depended on him; especially when I, out of punctilio

(And

(And was it punctilio?), would not go there till after my visit at North-End." I am very grateful, Madam, for that kind, though you call it punctilious visit; but let me say, that when I consented so cheerfully, to my own regret, to part with you so much sooner than you had intended to leave us, I think, as you staid so much longer at Ankerwyke than you designed, you might, in your return, have paid us back a day or two of the three or four we lent you, and given me then the opportunity to attend you to Enfield, which I had been deprived of to Ankerwyke. This would have been the least that we might have expected from a dutiful child. But the young lady that could not find time to write, in many weeks, one promised letter! Well!---I won't call you so much as a punctilious daughter. Yet I should not have said half so much, had I not been so strongly challenged for supposed defects, when my girl only was in fault. For, after all, I heartily rejoice that you were so much more delightfully entertained and diverted, than we could possibly

bly have diverted you.----Only you might have remembered one thing, that the rich in time and leisure you may have with you always.

And now, Madam, let me ask, can you forgive this scolding letter? If you can, I forgive you. But it is the part, it is the duty of a father, as you own, to tell his children of their faults. And now I have done scolding.

My best respects to my kind sister and friend, your ever-honoured mamma; in which joins my wife, as well as to you and Miss Betsey: and believe me to be,

My half, my almost-half, good girl,

Your truly affectionate and

Faithful humble servant,

S. RICHARDSON.

TO MR. RICHARDSON.

Enfield, Nov. 23, 1750.

AFTER writing my last to my dear papa, I, little thinking of any ill towards me, sat down pretty easy, and tolerably self-satisfied. I thought indeed you might complain of not hearing from me sooner; that I ought to have wrote while at Ankerwyke, if but two lines, to account for not writing more (for, as to the charge of deferring it after my return, I surely stand acquitted, since I sent a letter almost immediately; but this *en passant*): I, however, flattered myself, that the genuine account I gave in mine, how fully my time was taken up in my absence from hence, would, with my good papa (as I then thought you), have served rather for my excuse than as an aggravation of my faults real and supposed; when,

when, to my surprise, I find I had little reason to be thus tranquil!

I have been so much vexed, that I own I was very unwilling to answer it presently; for it was first necessary to work myself into an ill-humour, to be equal to the task: and as that must be a painful circumstance to myself, and all here, I endeavoured rather to think as little as possible of having received such a letter, or that it was necessary to write an answer to it. But patience will hold out no longer: my vexation rises to my pen; and, for relief, must throw itself off this way. I have heard of dipping one's pen in gall: O that I had a little gall by me now, instead of harmless ink! Do, pray, Sir, send me some against next time; as you have, I believe, to spare.

As to the word punctilio, I only meant, as I before said, that I scrupled going to Ankerwyke (though in the expectation of meeting you there; and consequently the pleasure had been the same at either place) till after my visit to North-End; it being surely first due there.

Thus far out of punctilio. Not that this could imply I had no other inducement to it; since, if I had no regard to that, nor yet to my promise given, as being a promise-breaker, my inclination would have prevailed most certainly over all. But what signifies writing, or attempting to explain, since I am not so happy as to be believed? And what, again, had I to do with hard words? Sure it will be a warning for me not to make use of another, as being liable to be so misunderstood.

I again ask pardon for detaining you that unfortunate Saturday so long in town: but should mistakes be imputed as design? A fault, I own, it was; and therefore beg forgiveness.

Then, for you, dear Sir; wherein do I blame you, if I dared presume to do it, unless my expressing, with undissembled concern, how grieved I was for not having your company down with me, or seeing you while there, is to be called blaming you?

I shall not endeavour to excuse my not calling at North-End in my way back, unless you will

will generously admit for an excuse the being in Mrs. Jodrell's coach, with herself in it, and she pressed for time, being to prepare for her journey into Hampshire, and but little to do it in: and this indeed is but another fact, which put it out of my power to revisit North-End, though but at two bow-shoots distance: nor knew I, if I could, whether my papa was there or not.

After all, I would never have written thus much, whether so very culpable as you think me or not (for I partly leave it to your determination to say what I am), but merely to convince you I was not intentionally faulty; and, whatever blunders have been made by me, I would hope to clear them up as far as I am able, choosing much rather you should at last censure the head, than the heart, of, dear papa,

Your still very affectionate,

yet hardly-treated,

S. WESTCOMB.

P. S. How have you teased me, you dear naughty Sir, you! My poor mamma, and all here, suffer for it. She asks me, what makes me so fretful and peevish? I answer, Papa. But as I have now emptied my poor quiver, I am again pretty well come to myself; and desire my mamma's and my duty, &c. may be accepted.

TO MISS WESTCOMB.

London, December 5, 1750.

ONLY, my dear Miss Westcomb, that paternal indulgence will ever get the better of paternal displeasure, or I should not be quite satisfied with yours of the 23d of November. Such a mixture!—Why, my dear, you give anger for anger! And yet I used, for the charming sweetness of your temper, as well as delicacy of your person, to call you my dove. Dove!

Dove! Yes, I say dove! But who knows what a lady is till she is provoked?

You are not in fault at all!—Not you!—Let me put a few questions to you?

Don't you think I love you dearly? With a love truly paternal?

You know I do, you answer. Yes, my dear, all that know me know I do.

And don't you know how solicitous I was to make an opportunity to attend you to Ankerwyke?

And had you not opportunity to write when Mrs. Jodrell retired to write? when Miss Johnson retired to write to her papa?—Will you say no? Did not the former good lady remind you that you should? My concern at your slight has made me inquisitive, I can tell you that. And what then could you want but inclination? And yet my pride (I am very proud I can tell you—and that very particularly of your favours) will hardly permit me to suppose it. Let me say, Madam, that though

though I may not deserve to be favoured, I cannot bear to be slighted.

What was Mrs. Jodrell's writing, to your promise of a letter, my dear girl? Answer me that,—Your voluntarily-promised letter? I thought you knew, that when we men obtain a promise of favour from a lady, we hold her to it----But I was but a papa!----Very well, Miss Westcomb!

Your pleasures at Ankerwyke?----Do you think I was not delighted to hear—to be told of your delights there? Indeed I most sincerely was. But would it not have been a still greater delight, think you, for me to have been told of those delights as you took them, that my imagination, though my person could not, might have shared them with you, than as delights actually past?

And would it not have been the highest and most acceptable of compliments to your papa, to find that you could withdraw yourself for one half-hour from the charming scenes and engagements

ments you describe, to perform—What?—Your promise?—Only your promise? That was all!

What is the tenor of your letter before me? Shall I give you an abstract of it? I will. Perhaps you have not kept a copy.

You own, in the first place, " That you thought indeed I might complain of not hearing from you sooner; that you ought to have wrote while at Ankerwyke, if but two lines, to account for not writing more." These are your own words: and yet I am guilty of a naughty ingenuity; as if I took a pleasure in torturing, mangling, perverting your meanings to my own disadvantage! Fine pleasure, truly! Fie, fie! is said to me; you never saw such a papa! Very well, child! You were so much vext, instead of sorry, that you own you were very unwilling to answer my letter. The word ' presently' interlined, as by an after-thought; by which it looks as if, in your dutiful wrath, you had
thoughts

thoughts of renouncing your poor papa! It was necessary, truly, you say, to work yourself into an ill-humour, to be equal to the task of answering my paternal complaints. Very fine indeed! But as this was likely to make every one about you suffer by the effects of that ill-humour (O dear! O dear!), you are resolved to forget you had received such a letter, or that it was necessary to write an answer (Was ever the like heard?). But patience would hold no longer:—your very words! And I had thought you a very dove for gentleness! But how, as I asked before, may one be mistaken in young ladies!—Your vexation (worse and worse!) rises to your pen. You wish for gall instead of ink! want to borrow some of me (there's dutifulness!)—What will young ladies come to, when not used to check or controul! when mother-indulged as you, my child, have been?

Then you rally me, truly, on my fears, my apprehensions, for your safety!—And yet I know

I know you to be near a forest where there was a great wild bear who had cubs to purvey for her devouring maw. I am accused for these fears, for these paternal fears, on your silence, and not knowing what had become of you; and whether you were still at the Forest, or returned to the neighbourhood of the Chace. I am accused of playing off a sheet full of witticisms (Witticisms, Miss W.! Very reverent indeed!), which you, poor girl, can't tell what to do with. Very well, Miss W. But I did not expect----But no matter----What have I done with my handkerchief? I----I----I did not expect----But no matter, Miss W.

Then comes a dissertation on the word punctilio, which you are resolved to renounce. I can't help it, my dear; one might indeed have expected that you would, after such neglects, and such a defence of yourself. You grudge to be called a promise-breaker. Yet, did you keep your promise, child? No; you pretend not to say you did. And what is your excuse?

excuse? Why, truly, you were so engrossed by your diversions (forbid it, paternal indulgence, that I should grudge my dear girl her diversions!), that you could not find one five minutes to write to me but two lines, to account for not writing more----In how many weeks?

You ask pardon about that Saturday. But what need at this distance? and when I had the happiness to find you at last where I had so long wished you to be?---Your goodness is not lost upon me.

At last, however, you have thought of a reason why you did not perform your promise in writing to me. And you are glad with all your heart, you say, that you did think of it: it was, because Mr. Jodrell wrote to me. A pretty excuse indeed! And Mr. Jodrell told you, I doubt not, that I answered him: that I was so unhappy as not to be able to accept, at that time, of his kind invitation. And you staid after that many weeks at Ankerwyke
against

against my expectation, and your own intention; and not one word did I hear either of my girl or her promise!

But your postscript concerns me more than all the rest. To think that your dear, your indulgent mamma should suffer for what you call (for what you own to be) your fretfulness, your peevishness, on this occasion; and when I told you too, that if you would excuse my scolding letter, I would excuse you, affects me.

Pray let me hear that by your redoubled duty you set all right with so tender a parent (and that from her goodness I know is soon done), or else you will add a concern to my heart, greater than even any you could give or have given to it by your neglects of,

My dear Miss Westcomb,

Your truly paternal friend,

S. RICHARDSON.

TO MR. RICHARDSON.

January 25, 1750-1.

DEAR SIR,

How could you desire me a second time to pain my mamma, and to pain you, only to pain poor me? This is cruelty, nay revenge; and shews you had rather sometimes smart a little yourself, than not tease another. Yet after all, I really believe I wanted but small encouragement to run into the saucy vein; and begin to fear there may lurk a spark of secret spite at the bottom of a certain heart; which, under a smooth outside, conceals roguery and mischief: upon my word, I should not before have suspected it, I hoped better of it, did not you, my good Sir? However, you know I am but a coward. and can only brave you out of your presence----all mild and gentle as it is.

On casting my eye over your letter I am really

really frighted. How many heavy charges are there brought against me! The weight is such it has almost borne me down, or at least bent me round-shouldered: for first, am I not taxed with writing in anger? Do you not upon it recall the sweet name of dove? And after a pause twice again repeat dove, to imply how greatly you have been mistaken in giving it me. What a pity you should so sadly throw your dove away! And I fear the poor creature is too far escaped me to be again lured back. Yet, if you should meet with the little fugitive, pray, good papa, restore her to me; for I cannot bear the thought of losing her for ever. I desire nothing more than a friend who would be impartial enough to make me see my errors: all that I beg is, that you'll bear with me not only with human, but with christian patience, since 'tis necessary here; and let me see, as I've shewn but little, that you greatly outdo me in this, as in every other excellence.

I find you have misinterpreted my reason for declining your kind offer, of going with
me

me to Ankerwyke in the way you proposed. I shall not dispute whether 'twas right in me or not; all that I can say is, you may depend upon it that nothing would have given me greater pleasure than your company on the journey, and truly sorry was I that at last I was deprived so unluckily. But now comes the formidable article of not writing after promise. Oh! what a terrible word! What shall I say? What can I say? Why nothing; but yet I think I could excuse it a little. Yet once more, self-justifier, be quiet—not another syllable: a promise broke is a promise broke, and nothing I can urge will make it less so. Well, if ever I go to Ankerwyke again, I will (Oh! bless me, here is another promise coming) sit up all night rather than not save my word; but even then I do not know how I shall keep it, for we never go to bed till late, and rise pretty early. Here let me ask, if you are not a naughty and undutiful papa, to tell me with a Madam, I cannot bear to be slighted? adding I know not what of favours, &c. Surprising!

prising! What a style is this to me! for pray, Sir, am I not your daughter? do I not owe infinite favours to you? I desire, Sir, in any succeeding epistles you may oblige me with, never to rob me of these words; they are properly mine, nor ought you to use them. I am very brave, you find, and 'tis impossible for you, dear Sir, to know otherwise, unless you were present, and could here behold me wiping my eyes. But then your triumph would be too complete. You had much occasion indeed to banter me (poor thing!) about a handkerchief. Well, do laugh at me; I love to have you merry, though at my expence, even tears and all. You may well call me an irreverent undutiful child for applying the terms naughty, ill-natured, and fie! fie! to my papa; but then is there to be no allowance made for one that has ever been mother-and father-indulged, unchecked, and uncontrolled to this day? Sure there is.---Then I am blamed for being vexed instead of sorry. To be ingenuous, I own I was both; for I was not only
concerned

concerned at your displeasure, but somewhat dissatisfied at your treatment, as thinking it rather severe than just. As to renouncing my papa! What, my own dear papa! Sure you could not believe any thing so hard of me, though you wrote it? And if I suspected you did, it would break my heart; and as it is, you surely think it very tough. But I know you suppose better of me, and only said it to vex me. I told you how fully my time was taken up while at Ankerwyke. I thought that common politeness required me to give my whole time to my friends while with them; but now, I am sensible that all considerations should have given way to my duty, my honour, or my word, which is in reality the same. All that I now beg is, that you'd be assured that you can never be, intentionally, neglected or slighted by, good Sir,

Your affectionate and filial friend,

and obliged humble servant,

S. WESTCOMB.

TO MISS WESTCOMB.

A LETTER from my dear was what I wished and hoped for, as my wife, by my last, could have shewn you: and I am greatly obliged that I had that favour spontaneously.

I thank you for your kind wishes for my health. You are absolutely right in judging that I had rather be in a desert, than in a place so public and so giddy, if I may call the place so from its frequenters. But these waters were almost the only thing in medicine that I had not tried; and as my disorders seemed to increase, I was willing to try them.—Hitherto, I must own, without effect is the trial. But people here, who slide in upon me, as I traverse the utmost edges of the walks, that I may stand in nobody's way, nor have my dizziness increased by the swimming triflers, tell me, I shall not give them fair play under a month or six weeks; and that I ought neither to write nor read—yet my my business as well as inclination compelling me to do a great deal of both. For I have all my town concerns upon me here, sent me every post and coach, and cannot help it.

Here are great numbers of people got together. A very full season, and more coming every day—Great comfort to me! When I say that I cannot abide them, nor the diversions of the place, you must not think that I am such a stoic as to despise the amusements I cannot partake of, purely on that account; indeed I do not. And I think youth is the season for gaiety. Nor is it a folly, as you are pleased to call it, in you, that you can find allurements in a brilliant circle, and at a sparkling ball.— But there is a moderation to be approved of in all these, which I see not here. And methinks I would wish that wives (particularly some that I see here) would not behave as if they thought themselves unmarried coquettes, and that it were polite to make their husbands the last persons in their notices. Is it not enough for these people to find themselves dressed and adorned,

adorned at an expense, both as to quality and quantity, that would furnish out two wives or mistresses: but they must show that those dresses and ornaments are bestowed upon them to please and delight any body rather than the person whom it should be their principal study to please; and who, perhaps, confers, or contributes to confer, upon them the means by which they shine, and think themselves above him? Secret history and scandal I love not— or I could tell you—you don't think what I could tell you.

But, waving these invidious subjects, what if I could inform you, that among scores of belles, flatterers, triflers, who swim along these walks, self-satisfied and pleased, and looking defiances to men (and to modesty, I had like to have said; for bashfulness seems to be considered as want of breeding in all I see here): a pretty woman is as rare as a black swan? And when one such starts up, she is nicknamed a Beauty, and old fellows and young fellows are set a-spinning after her.

Miss Banks (Miss Peggy Banks) was the belle when I came first down----Yet she had been so many seasons here, that she obtained but a faint and languid attention; so that the smarts began to put her down in their list of had-beens!----New faces, my dear, are more sought after than fine faces. A piece of instruction lies here,—that women should not make even their faces cheap.

Miss Chudleigh next was the triumphant toast: a lively, sweet-tempered, gay, self-admired, and, not altogether without reason, generally admired lady----She moved not without crowds after her. She smiled at every one. Every one smiled before they saw her, when they heard she was on the walk. She played, she lost, she won—all with equal good-humour. But, alas, she went off, before she was wished to go off. And then the fellows' hearts were almost broke for a new beauty.

Behold! seasonably, the very day that she went away entered upon the walks Miss L. of Hackney!—Miss Chudleigh was forgot (who

(who would wish for so transient a dominion in the land of fickledom!)—And have you seen the new beauty?—And have you seen Miss L.? was all the inquiry from smart to smartless—But she had not traversed the walks two days, before she was found to want spirit and life. Miss Chudleigh was remembered by those who wished for the brilliant mistress, and scorned the wife-like quality of sedateness—And Miss L. is now seen with a very silly fellow or two, walking backwards and forwards unmolested----dwindled down from the new beauty to a very pretty girl; and perhaps glad to come off so. For, upon my word, my dear, there are very few pretty girls here. And yet I look not upon the sex with an undelighted eye, old as I am; nor with a very severe one----But modesty, humility, graciousness, are now all banished from the behaviour of these public-place frequenters of the sex----Women are not what they were----I see not but they have as much courage as the men----The men, indeed, at these public places seem to like them the better for it.

it. No wonder; for they find the less difficulty to make parties with them, and to get into their companies----But one secret I could tell them; that the single men who would make the best companions for life, come not, on set purpose, to these public places to choose one.

But here, to change the scene, to see Mr. W—sh at eighty (Mr. Cibber calls him papa), and Mr. Cibber at seventy-seven, hunting after new faces; and thinking themselves happy if they can obtain the notice and familiarity of a fine woman!----How ridiculous!----If you have not been at Tunbridge, you may nevertheless have heard that here are a parcel of fellows, mean traders, whom they call touters, and their business touting---riding out miles to meet coaches and company coming hither, to beg their custom while here.

Mr. Cibber was over head and ears in love with Miss Chudleigh. Her admirers (such was his happiness!) were not jealous of him: but, pleased with that wit in him which they had not, were always for calling him to her.

She

She said pretty things—for she was Miss Chudleigh. He said pretty things—for he was Mr. Cibber; and all the company, men and women, seemed to think they had an interest in what was said, and were half as well pleased as if they had said the sprightly things themselves; and mighty well contented were they to be second-hand repeaters of the pretty things. But once I faced the laureat squatted upon one of the benches, with a face more wrinkled than ordinary with disappointment. "I thought," said I, "you were of the party at the tea-treats—Miss Chudleigh is gone into the tea-room"—"Pshaw!" said he, "there is no coming at her, she is so surrounded by the toupets"—And I left him upon the fret—But he was called to soon after; and in he flew, and his face shone again, and looked smooth.

He had written a dialogue between a father and daughter—the intention, to show that the paternal authority and filial obedience may be reconciled! He has read it to half a score at a time of the fair sex; and not a young lady but is mightily pleased with a lesson that will teach her to top her father. He read it to the Speaker and me. I made objections to it. I told him, that I saw he intended not to make his girl dutiful; but I besought him to let her be generous. The Speaker advised, that he should let me have it to look upon.— He insisted himself that I should give him some remarks upon it.—I did, upon the first page only; excusing myself as to the rest--- but, in short, the piece is calculated, as it stands at present, to throw down all distinction between parents and children.----Yet it has met with so much applause among the young flirts, that I don't know whether he will not publish it.----If he does, I had a good mind that Miss Howe (who is pert enough of conscience to her mamma; Clarissa you know is dead) should answer it.

Another extraordinary old man we have had here, but of a very different turn; the noted Mr. Whiston, showing eclipses, and explaining other phænomena of the stars, and preaching

preaching the millennium, and anabaptism (for he is now, it seems, of that persuasion) to gay people, who, if they have white teeth, hear him with open mouths, though perhaps shut hearts; and after his lecture is over, not a bit the wiser, run from him, the more eagerly to C---r and W----sh, and to flutter among the loud-laughing young fellows upon the walks, like boys and girls at a breaking-up.

You see, my dear, what a trifling letter I have written. You set me upon it. My head is very indifferent—my nerves no better than when I came down----and I should not write so much, they say, as I do----otherwise, if you could bear such stuff, I could run on a volume; relating others' follies and forgetting my own.---But 'tis time to relieve you, and to assure you that I am, with great gratitude and respect, my dear,

Your affectionate and paternal friend

and servant,

S. RICHARDSON.

TO MR. RICHARDSON.

Enfield, June 15, 1754

A Most agreeable favour will all here esteem it to see my dear papa, accompanied by as many of the good family as he pleases; and the earlier the day, the earlier shall we think ourselves happy. We should be glad of even a quarter of a line beforehand, lest, as is frequently the case, my mamma, &c. may be rode out for eighteen or twenty miles. How great then would be the disappointment! Thank you, dear sir, for stooping to pick me up again, if you had (as I feared) dropt me, for I could not reconcile myself to your travelling through the journey of life, without your now and then pointing me out by a finger the right path to take, for conducting me safely through it: then will it be my own fault, if I don't pursue it.---Some would ask, What necessity, or obligation, are you under to take

take this pains? I answer, The strongest that can be—the justification of yourself to your own heart, which, being perfect and good, requires that you should be, as you are, diffusively so, and the world in general become wiser and better by your means.

I, and all, sincerely lament your indispositions—may your nerves gain strength, but indeed they have been thoroughly tried, by study, application, and a tender feeling heart! Accept our best respects and wishes for the amendment of your health, and believe me, as ever,

Dear Sir, most affectionately,

your obliged friend and servant,

S. Westcomb.

TO MISS WESTCOMB.

London, October 22, 1754.

MY dear Miss Westcomb having written in her last excellent and affecting letter, that she would be glad to see me, as opportunity offered, at Enfield, or, when she came to town, in town; and not having expressed any immediate service that she could employ me in, I thought it was not amiss to wait till her grief for a loss so great and recent* was, as I may say, mellowed a little by the help of reflection;—not doubting but I should be favoured with her instant commands, if any thing offered that my assistance could be of use or comfort to her in. But I cannot excuse myself from inquiring by pen and ink, after the health of a daughter and friend so dear to me: and at the same time, from thanking you for a letter

---

* The death of Mrs. Westcomb.

so tender and pathetic; and to rejoice with you on a departure so resigned and happy.

You must not, my dear Miss Westcomb—so long a weaning-time allowed you, and so much suffered by the departed, and such resignation and piety shown—think too deeply of a loss, that, nevertheless, I will not offer to lessen in your dutiful mind. It is a great one. And I share it with you, as a brother to the deceased. But a lady of your discretion cannot have those dangers to apprehend on being sole, that hundreds of others, in the like case, would have. You may have trouble enough given you, as an independent person, by presumers: but your trials of that sort will be over in a few months; and none but the worthy (as I am sure what your conduct will be on those occasions) will dare to approach you. If others did, has not my dear Miss Westcomb a friend in every one who has the pleasure of being acquainted with her? Most cordially and paternally such is

Her ever faithful and affectionate,

S. Richardson.

TO MR. RICHARDSON.

Kentchurch, August 26, 1757.

A REMARKABLE day to me, viz. my wedding-day;—thank God, this is a happy one.

Though I have been here a week to-morrow, I have not had an opportunity of writing to my dear papa till now. The place quite new, and indeed every thing around me so; a large family, to the number of twenty-three, which require some attention; not to say that much of the time is taken up about my little boy, who, thank God, comes on apace, as the phrase is. I am agreeably surprised in finding Kentchurch very different from what has been represented: I was led to believe it was a sad forlorn dismal place, fit only to be inhabited by hobgoblins; but I declare, I have as yet neither heard or seen any thing but what has given me pleasure. The house 'tis true is old and irregular, part of it having been built, and

and in the family, before William the Conqueror: there are a great many good rooms: several of them have been fitted up, and furnished in a modern taste, by Mr. Scudamore, some time since; the rest may soon be put in proper conditions at a small expense. I was not a little surprised to find here so many conveniencies in kitchen, parlour, and hall, considering it was till now only occupied by a bachelor:—the cellars and vaults being well stored, is far less to be wondered at, as gentlemen are generally very provident on that article. The above was wrote some days ago, but I had not an opportunity to finish my letter, such a one as it is.

The weather has been so bad I have been out of doors but once, which would not permit me to make any judgment of the country round us; for the house is situated in a bottom. The park rises to a hill in the front, which is no sooner ascended than another rises above it; there is in a word no level ground about it. On Friday morning my my trusty knight conducted me to take a little survey of the premises. We first went through some beautiful meadows planted through, for a considerable length, with rows of trees; a river runs along on one hand, and the park lies on the other side of it, covered with a great number of spreading oaks, among which are cattle of different kinds grazing, and deer leaping over the fine turf. Before these meadows appears a most extensive prospect, all finely cultivated, with a great variety of grain; here and there are interspersed the ruins of old castles, antient family-seats, particularly one belonging to the Cecils, from whence the most renowned of that name is derived. A pretty spire of a church makes a point of view; numbers of reapers and gleaners enliven the whole: to say all in a word, I scarce ever saw a finer landscape. On the right hand are apple orchards filled with the noblest trees I ever saw, under which are sown different kinds of grain. Thus no part is lost. This place affords plenty of all provisions, I may say

say in abundance : fowls seven-pence a couple, ducks about the same price, and so of the rest.

We had a pleasant journey hither, through a delightful country, the face of it pretty much the same for a great part of the way as this about us. Thank God, we met with no ill accident: all arrived in health. We now and then stuck a little by the way from the narrowness of the roads, which we were obliged to make wider in places by a spade. I doubt not but it will give dear Mrs. R. great satisfaction to know, our little boy bore the fatigue as well as any of us.

Duty, love, and compliments, ever attend your household, from Mr. Scuda, and

Dear Sir,

your very affectionate,

obliged and obedient,

S. SCUDAMORE.

TO MRS. SCUDAMORE.

September 12, 1757.

MAY my dear, my worthy Mrs. and Mr. Scudamore see together many, very many, anniversary wedding-days! every succeeding one happier than the former.

I am charmed with your descriptions of the country, the landscapes, the prospects. What a painter you are! My wife, my girls, all congratulate you, your Mr. Scudamore, Miss Scudamore, and Miss Betsey, as well as I. But my girls, said I? Ah, my dear, one of them has followed your example: may it be as happily! Polly, last Tuesday, September the sixth, was married to a Mr. Ditcher, a surgeon of Bath—and would you have believed it, had I not told you? is to go, by the mother's consent, to reside at Bath: sets out next Friday. Now she begins to breathe in sighs, poor woman!—yet all her own doings. Had I been the proposer, distance would have been an insuperable objection.

You

You know, Madam, what a trembling figure I made at St. George's church, Hanover Square, a year ago, when I was favoured with the opportunity of giving to Mr. Scudamore the most valuable jewel he could receive. This was urged upon me by way of engaging me in the same solemn office: and my consciousness of bad behaviour then, I would fain have made my excuse. But, cruel! it was not admitted; and very nervously affected for many weeks before, I have been grievously ill ever since; for some days unable to hold a pen; yet cared not, in hopes of one qualifying hour, as this, to suffer any body to write for me to my dear Mrs. Scudamore, though she gave me gracious leave to employ another in the pleasing task.

Every good wish attend you and yours from all mine, and from, Madam,

Your truly affectionate

and faithful humble servant,

S. RICHARDSON.

TO MR. RICHARDSON.

MY DEAR SIR,
                    Kentchurch, March 12, 1758.

I WAS, and still am, greatly affected by your last favour; though I own it cost me some tears, yet they were such as I liked to shed. Your great tenderness and affection for me; the difficulties you put yourself to in writing to me, from your ill-health, &c. touched my heart, and I burst into tears. "What's the matter?" asks my dear Mr. Scudamore: "you seem moved." "See here," replied I, "a letter from Mr. Richardson: so tender, so affectionate! Say, ought he not to be my real father, by his kind partiality for me? Indeed, I should blush to show a letter with so many encomiums on myself; but as 'tis another instance of the goodness of his heart." "Dear worthy man!" replied he, after perusing it."
"God

" God long preserve the most worthy of men!"
An amen closed the conversation; being rather too tender to continue it longer.

I've lately read over my oracle (Pamela) again, and already made use of some of Mr. Locke's maxims, made clear and plain by her, upon my little boy, which I highly approve, and intend strictly to adhere to. If there is already any judgment to be formed, he is of a good disposition; he laughs, plays, and almost runs alone. I shall ever take a pleasure, nay think it my duty, to teach him, and all around me, to respect and love your character; and hope, before a great while elapses, to bring him to know you in person; and to ask your blessing. I will not despair in due time of seeing you here. Change of place, different air, &c. and a hearty welcome, may perhaps be of service. Let us entreat you (if possible) to make trial of it.

I have been of late pretty much at home, but have almost constantly had some family or other with me. A great many of the nobility and

and gentry, of the county, are very agreeable people, and do me an honour and pleasure in entering into a friendship with me. But I am really a sad body to run on so much of self.

    Yours, &c.

      S. SCUDAMORE.

END OF THE THIRD VOLUME.

R. Taylor, Black horse Court

For EU product safety concerns, contact us at Calle de José Abascal, 56–1°,
28003 Madrid, Spain or eugpsr@cambridge.org.

www.ingramcontent.com/pod-product-compliance
Ingram Content Group UK Ltd.
Pitfield, Milton Keynes, MK11 3LW, UK
UKHW040613010525
458010UK00017B/16